Praise for Susan Peszneck
Crafting Magick with Pen and Ink

"A fine series of exercises, tips, and writing samples . . . Highly recommended."

—*Midwest Book Review*

"Whether you're writing nonfiction, fiction, or ritual material, there's plenty to love about this resourceful text."

—Lupa, *Thorn* magazine

"This book is a delightful and informative guide that has the added bonus of being Pagan-centric. Along with useful tips for the up-and-coming pro, all of which are presented in an original way, Pesznecker also offers inspiration for those who wish to write for themselves . . . I highly recommend it both to those seeking a career in writing and to creative types hoping to add life to journals, prayers, spells, and rituals."

—*SageWoman* magazine

"In this book, [Pesznecker] creates a gentle amalgam of magick and grammar . . . As I finish reading *Crafting Magick with Pen and Ink*, I see that telling stories is another style of casting spells."

—Diana Page Jordan, journalist and author

"Whether you are in the brainstorming phase of the writing process or just need an extra little push to finish your masterpiece, *Crafting Magick with Pen and Ink* can give you the motivation and inspiration you need to live up to your literary potential."

—*E-Witch* book reviews

The Magickal Retreat

About the Author

Susan Pesznecker is a mother, writer, nurse, hearth Pagan, and Druid living in northwest Oregon. She teaches writing and literature at Portland State University and Clackamas Community College. In her spare time, she practices organic gardening, green magick, and herbalism, and she loves to read, take long walks with her wonder poodle, camp, play with rocks, and spend time in the outdoors. She teaches green magick at the online Grey School (www.greyschool.com) and is also the author of *Gargoyles* (New Page Books, 2007) and *Crafting Magick with Pen and Ink* (Llewellyn, 2009).

You can contact Susan via her webpage, www.susanpesznecker.com. *Ex amino . . .*

Susan Pesznecker

The Magickal Retreat

Making Time for Solitude,
Intention & Rejuvenation

Llewellyn Publications
Woodbury, Minnesota

First Edition
First Printing, 2012

Book design by Donna Burch
Cover art: Labyrinth Petaluma: John Glover/Garden Picture Library/Photolibrary
        Grunge banner: iStockphoto.com/Christina Veit
Cover design by Lisa Novak
Interior banner: iStockphoto.com/Christina Veit

Llewellyn is a registered trademark of Llewellyn Worldwide Ltd.

Library of Congress Cataloging-in-Publication Data
Pesznecker, Susan.
  The magickal retreat : making time for solitude, intention & rejuvenation / Susan Pesznecker. — 1st ed.
      p. cm.
  Includes bibliographical references (p.   ) and index.
  ISBN 978-0-7387-3066-0
1. Spiritual retreats. I. Title.
  BL628.P47 2012
  204'.46—dc23
                    2012003248

Llewellyn Publications
A Division of Llewellyn Worldwide Ltd.
2143 Wooddale Drive
Woodbury, MN 55125-2989
www.llewellyn.com

Printed in the United States of America

Other books by this author

Crafting Magick With Pen and Ink: Learn to Write Stories, Spells and Other Magickal Works

Gargoyles: From the Archives of the Grey School of Wizardry

Dedication and Acknowledgments

This book is happily dedicated to my teachers and my students, both magickal and mundane, who push me to challenge myself. It's dedicated to Joseph Campbell, whose brilliance continues to spark generations of seekers. It's dedicated to my friends, who have provided boundless support and encouragement—especially Carol and Monique and their "sprints." Most of all, it's dedicated to my family. Without my mother, my incredible children, and even my trusty wonder poodles to inspire me, I wouldn't have been able to accomplish this work nor would I be where I am today. I love them, and I'm grateful they love me, too.

Contents

Part V: Afterword

Part VI: Resources

Foreword

How to Use This Book

In this book, we'll explore the idea of personal retreat, considering the benefits that come from temporarily pulling out of the mainstream and looking deeply within oneself. We'll examine the historic (and magickal!) roots of these concepts, the benefits you'll gain from a retreat experience, and several strategies for planning and carrying out your own spectacular personal retreat.

This book is organized for easy use. In Part I, "The Seeker and the Lore of the Retreat," you'll read an introduction to the ideas and lore of the personal retreat, and you'll explore the quintessential "hero's journey" that underpins the themes in this book. Part II, "Heeding the Call," begins the process of planning a retreat and considering the details that will be part of it. In Part III, "Departure, Initiation, and Return," you'll be guided in not only launching your retreat but also evaluating it afterward. Part IV—"Individual Retreat Plans"—provides a set of ready-to-use retreat templates as well as a host of ideas to use in developing your own getaways. Finally, Parts V and VI, "Afterword" and "Resources," provide further inspiration and hands-on materials to help you see the experience through.

Depending on your background and magickal experience, I'd like to offer the following suggestions for working with this book:

- **If you're new or somewhat new to magick practice**, I'd suggest you read the entire book through from beginning to end. The book follows the "hero's journey" from start to finish; not only will it lead you, step by step, through the process of planning, creating, and carrying out a personal retreat, but you'll also pick up a number of important magickal skills and techniques along the way—and you'll be put in touch with a number of terrific magickal resources. At the end of each chapter, a set of tasks will help you reflect on what you've just covered and will help you apply the material to your own potential retreat.

- **If you're an experienced magickal practitioner and want to jump straight into the retreat itself,** I suggest you begin by reading chapters 1 and 2, as they explore the "why" of the retreat and provide the "journey" context that is referenced throughout the book. The material in these chapters provides food for thought and is intended to make your experience richer and more meaningful. After reading those two chapters, you might head for Part IV, "Individual Retreat Plans"; this section provides ready-to-go retreats and ideas, allowing you to move quickly into your own retreat experience. Check Appendix C in Part VI, "Magickal Resources for Your Retreat," for supporting materials. And you might want to peruse Appendix D, as even the most experienced practitioner can benefit from considering the role of mentoring in his or her life.

- **Do you love to plan? Are you detail-oriented?** Working through the book from start to finish will provide a step-wise, logical guide to retreat craft and will take you—efficiently—from point A to point Z. You'll read, you'll journal, you'll plot, and you'll finish with a strong retreat plan in hand and all the tools you need to undertake it.

- **Are you more of a "seat of your pants" person? More of a grab-and-go mage?** Review chapter 7, which explains the basics of arranging a retreat plan. Then skip to Part IV, scanning the sample retreats until you find an idea or outline that appeals to you. I'd still encourage you to read chapters 1 and 2, as they'll give you some excellent background for what retreat is and why we do it. Chapter 9 might be useful, too—it will help you consider the aftermath of the retreat and the reflective details that are very important but easy to overlook. Grab a pencil and dig in!

- **Regardless of your starting point**, be sure to read through chapter 6, "Solitude and Mindfulness." This chapter has a lot to say about the essential nature of sequestering oneself, as well as discussing the value of intention and mindfulness to your retreat experience.

A few more details, before we begin:

Although this book will be useful for anyone, the correspondences and seasons within correspond with the northern hemisphere. If you live in the southern hemisphere, you'll want to adjust accordingly.

While this book is aimed at a single person undergoing a private retreat, there are times when a group—a circle, coven, grove, or other group—may desire to retreat together in order to accomplish a specific purpose. I'll discuss group retreats in chapter 21; if this applies to you, give it a look.

This book is designed to be used and used actively. Read with a pen or pencil in hand, underlining, circling, and writing comments in the margins as you go. This kind of interaction effectively enters you into a discussion *with* the book, and will make the experience that much richer. It'll also ensure that you don't forget important details as you read.

Many blessings to you, and happy reading!

During sessions of solitude, periods of silence, or "time retreats," we shun life's chattering distractions and simply notice what is left: ourselves.

—HELEN CORDES

Part I

The Seeker
and the
Lore of
the Retreat

The intuitive mind is a sacred gift and the rational mind is a faithful servant.
We have created a society that honors the servant and has forgotten the gift.

—ALBERT EINSTEIN

Chapter One

The Need for Retreat

Beware the barrenness of a busy life.
—SOCRATES

It's a busy world we live in. Juggling families, jobs, school, recreation, and social lives, we tend to pack so much into each day that we often find ourselves either shoe-horning magick and spirituality into the last fifteen minutes before we collapse or putting them off altogether with a promise to readdress on the morrow. But then the next day comes and the same thing happens again. Before we know it, a week or a month or even an entire season has passed, and we realize how thoroughly we've neglected our spiritual selves.

None of this is new—we humans have always been busy people. Many argue that the digital age has catapulted us into new levels of hyper-scheduled 24/7 craziness, but in truth, there's always been something people can point to standing between them and their spiritual expression. I may have an electronic world to interact and deal with, but my grandmother had to kill dinner and make her own soap, for Goddess' sake. Each generation has had its own knot of distractions, keeping people from those things they *really* want to be doing, and some of that is never going to go away. After all: most of us have to work, and we choose to care for our families and friends and pets and covenmates. Those tasks can bring great joy. But they can also be exhausting, even numbing at times.

The problem comes when we fill our days and pack our schedule with "shoulds" and "musts" and "expectations" at the expense of practices that nurture our hearts and souls. The world intrudes, and it often asks more of us than we have the time or energy to give. Yet, we keep giving. We work hard, manage home and family, care for friends and loved ones, and check off long lists of scheduled obligations. The result is that time seems to accelerate. One of the realizations I've had in my adulthood is that when weeks and months suddenly seem to have flown by with nothing to show for them but a crammed datebook and a few paychecks, and I can't remember what I had for breakfast yesterday let alone what I did last week, something is wrong. It's at these times that many of us realize how much of our personal—and magickal—lives have been put on the back burner. As Einstein so aptly put it, the servant is working hard, but the gift has been forgotten. Or at least neglected.

Here's the thing: magick and spirituality need the best of us—not the last fifteen minutes of the day or a spot of time every couple of weeks. Magick needs concentration, intention, and time. It needs forethought and carefulness. Spirituality requires emotional "space" and readiness in order to provide a footing for communing with one's inner voice and one's gods and goddesses. Good magick needs us to step out of time and into liminal space, and we must do this with an open heart and the time and desire to receive whatever gifts are given. Can we do this if we're stressed? Exhausted? Numb? No, we certainly can't.

What's to be done? It's actually quite simple. Each of us must harness intention and decide that our spiritual lives will be a priority. To make a change like this requires stepping out of what has become routine and pushing the "restart" button. A wonderful way to do this is through the practical journey of *retreat.*

Think back to the last time that several unfilled, unplanned, unscheduled hours suddenly appeared in front of you, ready to be plucked. Perhaps your children had just returned to school, leaving you a glorious, quiet day. Maybe your husband went off on his annual hunting trip, leaving you home alone. Or maybe you found yourself snowed in, roads closed and work canceled for the day. Can you remember how that felt? How precious it felt to suddenly hear that call of silence and feel the schedule drift away? No doubt you were seized with possibilities. Would you brew a cup of tea and sink into a book? Go for a long walk and treat yourself to a restaurant lunch? Head for a day at the beach? Or maybe you're the industrious type, rolling up your sleeves and tackling a disordered closet.

The point is, you seized the chance to do something for yourself. In stepping out of your daily routine and schedule, you embraced possibility. You reveled in the un-planned. Most importantly, you cared for yourself. Perhaps your mind cleared and settled enough that you thought about your spirituality or craft. Maybe you even worked some magick . . .

Humans have long used the idea of retreat, cloister, sanctuary, vigil, and quest to take these metaphorical steps out of "real time," entering the place where magick and spirituality are again possible. Once in this sacred space, we might relax, re-flect, meditate, rejoice, ponder, test, or even initiate ourselves, but whatever we do, we inevitably celebrate the opportunity to slow down and pay attention to our own spiritual needs.

Let's consider the idea of retreat more closely. The word *retreat* comes from the Latin *retrahere*, "to pull back or withdraw," and in times past, the retreat was most often linked to the idea of religious cloister. Religious clergy, acolytes, or postulants secluded themselves for spiritual instruction, immersion, and discipline. Retreat and cloister became linked to sanctuary and safety, with the retreating person seques-tered (literally, "committed for safekeeping") from the outside world. In medieval times, churches operated under their own laws, often separate from those of the sur-rounding land, and a lawbreaker in the real world could seek sequestered asylum and sanctuary within the walls of a church or cathedral. Once the fugitive reached the church walls and knocked with the *Hagoday* (a stylized door knocker), he was safe and received sanctuary under tenets of canonical law. Even today, retreat and sanctu-ary carry the *gestalt* of separating and protecting the participant from "worldly time."

Vigil is another concept commonly linked to retreat. Rooted in the Latin *vigilia*, "to keep awake," the traditional use of the word *vigil* is applied to one who stays awake for a long period with the intention of accomplishing a task or experiencing a revela-tion. The practices of medieval knights included vigil. Those selected for knighthood stayed awake through a long night, "watching by their arms"—their armor and weap-ons—and praying in the local church. The next morning, the king or lord knighted them and they were welcomed with great celebration and feasting. The vigil became the culmination of a classical hero's quest, in which the seeker had completed a long journey, surmounted a period of testing, and returned triumphant to be recognized with new status, a new name, and "boons," gifts and knowledge that supported the quester's new competence.

The ideas of quest, journey, and retreat also take root in the search for paradise, and ancient peoples often referred to the spectacular or mysterious in nature as supernatural. Deep canyons, soaring cliffs, frozen glaciers, and spinning tornadoes must surely have been created by the hand of one or more gods. Certain natural settings took on positive or malignant symbolism; the forest, for example, was often regarded as a place of dark chaos, a place where one could be swallowed up—literally eaten. As civilizations developed and societies formed, an early move common to all of them was to cut down the forests and replace them with ornate farms and gardens. In this way, the "forest primeval" was conquered and subdued—evil was managed. It's no coincidence that when humans imagine what paradise must be like, it's most often viewed as a kind of beautiful, manicured garden. The word *paradise* comes ultimately from the Old Persian *pairidaeza* and references a magical garden surrounding the holy mountain of the gods, where the Tree of Life bore the fruit of immortality. The Garden of Eden is another well-known expression of the garden paradise. Many quests and journeys in some way involve a search for this perfect place—for "paradise on Earth."

The hero's journey is a profound metaphor that infuses every magickal path and ties closely in with the ideas of retreat and self-sequester. The writer and comparative mythologist Joseph Campbell is credited for his work in identifying the common threads winding throughout world mythology and tradition as well as linking these under a common idea, which he called the monomyth. Campbell used this structure to define and explain the hero's journey, a theme that appears over and over throughout ancient and modern literature, art, music, dance, and storytelling—as well as in all types of retreat and quest. The hero's journey model also permeates various magickal traditions, including the Tarot and all forms of magickal training, e.g., the well-known "year and a day" common to structured forms of study.

We'll delve deeper into the quest model in chapter 2, but the following is a quick overview. In Campbell's work, the hero's journey invariably involves some sort of magickal descent into a place of "darkness," and many expressions of quest in art, film, and story find the hero wandering, wide-eyed into a dark forest, cave, or some sort of underworld. Campbell's theories incorporate a great deal of Carl Jung's (pronounced "Yoong's") work with the human psyche and collective unconscious—the idea that we're all born with "memories" of a shared past, and that these memories may surface with powerful results. Campbell also relied on Jung's work with mythic archetypes: the recurrent appearances of warrior, mother, Goddess, sage, fool, and other stock players that surface in every culture's myths and in every hero's journey. In the hero's eyes, all paths lead to home—a place that feels like paradise, given the perils of the road behind.

These concepts coalesce in the idea of personal retreat. We speak of "going on retreat" as a way to answer a call, slip away from the stream of society, and withdraw into temporary seclusion, solitude, and perhaps even silence. Chess pieces retreat from forward or threatened positions; we humans retreat from life's onslaughts or seclude ourselves to grapple with challenges and transitions. We retreat as an intentional means of pulling back, looking inward, and creating the personal time and space needed for rejuvenation. Philosopher Rudolf Steiner called this a meeting with the *ens astral*, a soul-filling connection with place and cosmos created through time, familiarity, and meditation. These sorts of magickal bonds don't happen without hard work and without creating intentional time and space. The value of the personal retreat is in its expression as a small—but very real—journey. Each retreat becomes a hero's quest as we respond to a challenge, set foot to path, test or try ourselves, look inward, and return, jubilant, to receive our own boons and revel in our new knowledge or accomplishment.

Let's get back to those ideas about being caught up in the rat race, the hamster wheel, the treadmill, or whatever metaphor you care to use. Each of these uses up time and energy. We're left feeling stressed, and we never really seem to get anywhere. As magickal folks, we find ourselves wistfully imagining having the time to read that new book or delve into a study of the runes or finish the cloak we started embroidering two years earlier . . .

Time for a change.

In the pages to follow, I'll help you push that restart button. I'll help you craft your own magickal retreat—a personalized intentional process in which you prepare to withdraw from the mundane world and set out on your own journey. It will be a chance to slow down and look inward. You'll use the time to rest, energize, and reboot your spiritual practices. You'll give yourself a chance to pause and reflect on what you've learned, where you stand right now, and what you want to do in the months and years to come. It might provide a chance to test or challenge yourself or to examine some aspect of yourself or your practices. It should also be a time to do something fun.

Let me mention something else. You may be one of the lucky ones who has already jumped off the hamster wheel and feels that your magickal and mundane lives are already in synch. If so, congratulations! But please understand that this book is still for you, too. Everyone can benefit from occasionally slowing down; doing some good, hard self-appraisal; and setting aside self-dedicated time. Whatever it is that's making you look to the idea of personal retreat, you'll benefit from the ideas in this book. Taking a retreat can open you to discovery, personal growth, and a chance to try something new. You can't help but grow in wisdom and joy through this kind of intentional experience. You'll bask in luxurious "me" time—and you're likely to have fun as well.

Are you ready? The seeker is one who searches, and the seeker's curiosity leads to new discoveries. Each discovery generates challenges, and each challenge—well met—builds wisdom. The first step begins here, with your first set of tasks.

Tasks for Chapter 1

At the end of each chapter, I'll provide several tasks to help you engage with the material as you work toward your own magickal retreat. These tasks will also guide you in the pathwork that follows your own hero's journey.

I suggest you make notes directly on these pages—annotating a book as you read is a powerful way to engage with its content—but I'd also advise you to begin a special retreat journal or diary—or, if preferred, that you use a magickal journal already in progress. As you work through the steps in this book, make notes and respond to exercises in your journal. I've left you some space after each of the "Tasks" to capture your ideas.

Read these questions aloud to yourself, and then write your responses:

1. What are some of the most important things I have learned about myself since I began studying magick or magickal spirituality? How was I first called to this path?

_____

_____

_____

_____

2. What new magickal skills or knowledge have I acquired since I began this journey?

_____

_____

_____

_____

3. What are my strengths and talents as a member of this path or practice? What are my weaknesses? What challenges do I face?

_____

_____

_____

_____

4. What subjects or practices do I want to explore more deeply?

_____

_____

_____

_____

5. How has my magickal growth contributed to myself? My family? My spiritual community?

_____

_____

_____

_____

6. How have I given back?

_____

_____

_____

_____

7. What have I put on the back burner in terms of my magickal self? If I had an extra half hour each day, what would I do more of?

_____

_____

_____

_____

Notes and Ideas

_____

_____

_____

_____

Chapter Two

Types of Retreat, or "Every Journey Is a Hero's Journey"

A hero ventures forth from the world of common day into a region
of supernatural wonder: fabulous forces are there encountered
and a decisive victory is won: the hero comes back from this mysterious
adventure with the power to bestow boons on his fellow man.

—JOSEPH CAMPBELL

As mentioned in chapter 1, each unique retreat is a mini-journey of sorts, and the hero's journey is an important model for this kind of experience. Why is this important? The hero's journey is filled with real metaphors that touch every human culture and every piece of mythos, past and present. By being aware of your connection to this magickally infused history, you connect with both the timeless and the divine, making your retreat experience all the richer.

Before we go further, let's take a quick look at a simplified structure of the hero's journey. Joseph Campbell, in his book *The Hero with a Thousand Faces*, divides the full schema into three main sections and seventeen separate components. I'm going to use J. R. R. Tolkien's *The Lord of the Rings* as an example throughout to illustrate the points; it's a book/film series most magickal folks are familiar with, and even if you're not, you'll be able to see a clear example of Campbell's model. This is my own summary/interpretation of Campbell's work; the reader is referred to his works, particularly *The Hero with a Thousand Faces*, for a more detailed examination. Note that while your own retreat journey may not include each of these components, it's still interesting and useful to see how the entire schema works together.

Phase I: The Departure

The hero is called to destiny and departs for the journey.

This is the phase of preparation; in your retreat, the period in which you plan, make arrangements, and set out on the journey coincides with Campbell's "departure" phase.

Campbell's Label	Description	Example
The Call to Adventure	The seeker receives a call to destiny or comes to understand that she has a destiny, cause, or task to fulfill.	*The One Ring comes to Frodo.*
Refusal of the Call	The seeker typically refuses the call at least once. She may not believe it, may not believe it possible, may be afraid of undertaking it, or simply may not care to accept it. Or, she might be "too busy." (Which is why we're here, right?)	*Frodo tries to give the Ring to Gandalf. Gandalf explains to Frodo that he must carry the Ring away from Hobbiton.*
Supernatural Aid	Once the call is accepted, the seeker receives guidance from a mentor; this guidance may be magickal, spiritual, mundane/ practical, or a combination of all three.	*Gandalf provides supernatural aid to Frodo. Gandalf and Aragorn will both serve as mentors to Frodo.*

Campbell's Label	Description	Example
Crossing the Departure Threshold	The seeker sets foot on the path and crosses a threshold, stepping into the "new" and entering magickal or liminal space.	*Frodo and Sam leave Hobbiton, bound for the town of Bree and, eventually, for the perils of Mordor.*
The Belly of the Whale	At some point, the seeker finds herself descending or cast into a place of darkness, or challenge. This space may be magickal or mundane. It may also be metaphorical; sometimes the test is something she must meet within herself.	*Along the road, the Hobbits are attached by Black Riders. Once in Bree, they meet Aragorn. Gandalf has vanished and Frodo begins to realize the seriousness of his journey. In Rivendell, Frodo shoulders the burden of returning the Ring to Mordor—his quest begins.*

Phase II: Initiation

The hero is tested and succeeds.

This is the "action" portion of the journey; for you, the period in which you carry out your retreat and reap the benefits coincides with Campbell's "initiation" phase.

Campbell's Label	Description	Example
The Road of Trials	Along the road, the seeker meets many trials. Each requires him to demonstrate growing skills, confidence, and maturity.	*The Fellowship is formed and begins the journey to Mordor. Frodo meets and undergoes many trials and challenges.*
Meeting with the Goddess/ God	The seeker receives some sort of direct spiritual or magickal insight or support; this will inspire him when the going gets rough. Often, the Goddess or God gifts the seeker with magickal information or objects.	*Frodo meets the Elf Queen and receives a vision of what will happen should he fail. He comes to better understand the import of what he must do. She also gives him a magick light to help him see in the darkest places. In other words, she gives him hope.*

Campbell's Label	Description	Example
Temptation Away from the True Path	As the road becomes more difficult, the seeker considers abandoning the quest and heading home. He may question the value of the quest or might deny that he is on the correct path or is capable of finishing it. He may be afraid or filled with doubt.	*On several occasions, Frodo is tempted to put on the Ring and allow Sauron to find him. It would be easier for him to end the arduous journey than to continue.*
Atonement with the Mother/Father	The seeker achieves enough competence to show he no longer needs the guidance of a mentor. The student has become the teacher, and the seeker's success is now in his own hands.	*Faramir allows Frodo and Sam to continue their journey. Frodo has now been set fully apart—from Bilbo, Gandalf, his village, Gollum, and the Fellowship—to succeed or fail on his own.*
Apotheosis—becoming "god-like"	The seeker appears to be innately strong, powerful, and capable. Others will look to or follow him without question. To the opposing forces, the seeker now represents great danger.	*Frodo becomes increasingly resolute as he grows closer to Mount Doom.*
The Ultimate Boon	The seeker achieves his quest and is gifted with new powers, skills, understandings, knowledge, and so on.	*Frodo stands within Mount Doom. As a result of his struggles with Gollum, the One Ring is cast into the molten lava and order is restored to Middle Earth.*

Phase III: The Return

The hero returns, and the quest—a rite of passage—is completed.

In your case, the period *after* the retreat—in which your return to the mundane world, consider how you've benefited, and evaluate the results—coincides with Campbell's "return" phase.

Campbell's Label	Description	Example
Refusal of the Return	The seeker may question her ability to return. Exhausted from her quest, she may feel that she is now so far outside her own imagined reality that return is impossible—i.e., there's no going back.	*Frodo and Sam perch on a rocky outcropping as molten lava streams around them. Sensing their death is near and believing that survival is impossible, they surround themselves with memories of home.*
The Magick Flight	The seeker receives magickal aid with her return. (Imagine Dorothy clicking her heels together three times . . .)	*Frodo and Sam escape death at Mount Doom when Gandalf sends the Eagles to pluck them off the rocks and carry them to safety.*
Rescue from Without	Outside forces assist the seeker's return.	*Frodo and Sam are rescued by the Eagles. (The giant birds, not the band.) Their triumph at Mount Doom is made possible when Aragorn's army keeps the enemy busy at the gates of Mordor.*
Crossing the Return Threshold	The seeker returns to her home and/or people, coming back to where she began. She leaves the "other" world and returns to what is familiar.	*The Hobbits—and the Fellowship—return to safety and to their corner of Middle Earth. Having returned to the familiar, life is once again as it should be.*

Campbell's Label	Description	Example
Master of the Two Worlds	She is now "more" than when she began. Joy, ceremony, and celebration are typically part of this stage, but there is also an inevitable loss of innocence, and sometimes a poignant sorrow.	*Both Sam and Frodo have finished a quest, and both have lost their innocence. They have seen and done things that most Hobbits never will, and they cannot "un-see" or undo those events. They are different from the way they were before the journey. They now know what both real and "other" worlds are like, and they can make a choice about how to live their lives.*
Freedom to Live	Because of the seeker's successful journey, the world benefits. The seeker's new role is to lead, teach, and inspire. Having mastered both worlds, she is now able to choose her own path. One day, she will mentor others in their own quests.	*Because of Frodo and the Fellowship's courage, the world of men survives, and the races of Middle Earth stand newly unified in their search for peace and well-being. Frodo chooses to leave the living world and sail off to the Undying Lands, having become master of both. Frodo's legacy lives on.*

As I mentioned in chapter 1, Campbell's work leans heavily on work done by psychiatrist Carl Jung, particularly with Jung's work in the "collective unconscious," a belief that we are all linked across time by a cosmic thread of shared human experience and that we're all born intuitively understanding these shared experiences. This explains why myths, rituals, and shared stories resonate so deeply within us—they help us tap into the deep magick, a sense of something much older than ourselves, and they help us find our own places within those stories. Looking at the above schema will suggest how your own experience might parallel the quest experience, making your retreat all the richer. You, too, will hear and answer the call. You'll set foot on the road, listen for magickal guidance, and test yourself in various ways. Tasks completed, you'll "return" as someone who is *different* from who you were when you began.

Campbell's ideas may give you specific ideas for making your retreat even more special, and we'll talk more about this as we work through the steps to come. For now, let's consider a few possibilities for retreat . . .

Seclusion

The simplest retreat of all is seclusion, and most retreats include some component of "alone time." To be secluded is to slip away, close one's self off from the mainstream, and settle into a private space. Time, schedules, and outside influences fade away . . . One of the seclusions many of us are familiar with is a hot bath with lots of candles, a good book, and a locked door. Long walks may fill the bill for some people, camping and remote vacations for others. The key seems to be finding a way to truly be alone, free from schedules, demands, and interruptions. A weekend getaway to a secluded spot may be just what you need to hear your own inner voice.

And while we're discussing it . . . I also believe that distancing oneself from electronic media—such as laptop, cell phone, and text messaging—is a vital aspect of seclusion for most people; this is something we'll talk more about later.

Sanctuary, Retirement, and Haven

Do you feel like you're actively trying to escape or remove yourself from something or someone? Perhaps you aren't happy with your job; one of your covenmates is driving you nuts; you just ended a difficult relationship; or you're weary from the demands of your family—even though you love them to death. The thing you may need most is to feel safe and untouchable. How can you craft a retreat that gives you this luxury? The ideas of "sanctuary" and "haven" lend themselves to works with magickal separation, removal, boundary setting, bond-cutting, and the like. These are also good choices if you're stepping down from a position of responsibility and looking for a meaningful transition.

Vigil, Observance, and Watchkeeping

I was involved in a vigil once, as part of my induction into a secret camping society. The vigil involved staying up through the night and maintaining a campfire under the open sky. As I sat by the fire, unseen voices from the trees around the fire would ask me questions—testing me. At dawn, I was welcomed into a new fold, gifted with a new name and a piece of regalia, and taken to enjoy a bounteous feast with the other members. What a welcome that was . . . (And then I went home and slept for fourteen hours!)

If you're completing a journey, finishing a time of testing, or contemplating some sort of progression or initiation in your practices, a retreat that includes vigil might be just the thing. The act of staying up through the night is powerful, as it links us to ancient times and transformative ritual, providing a satisfying feeling of completion. It may also represent the final step—and the final test—in a rite of passage, a process that results in personal growth, new awareness, and the loss of innocence that accompanies passage from one life-place to another.

New versions of "vigil" are constantly taking form in today's magickal society. For instance, many of those calling themselves modern alchemists have developed a practice known as the alchemical fire circle. Participants gather in remote locations to stage highly ritualized fire circles around which they dance vigil through the night. In these cases, the motivations for vigil are similar to those of the traditional silent watchkeeping, but the vigil instead is made of transformative fire, dance, and passion. Interesting, yes?

Vision Quest

Like vigil, a vision quest implies a period of remaining awake and alert for magickal purposes. The traditional vision quest also suggests some type of seeking. The quester may meditate or enter a trance state in hopes of being visited by spirits or a totem animal, receiving spiritual books or gifts, having a question answered, or perhaps discovering a new name. This is a powerful type of retreat experience for the person seeking inspiration or discovery. Like the vigil, the vision quest also typically represents a rite of passage.

Practice, Testing, and Trial

Most of us have one or more magickal skills that we'd like to be better at or wish we had more time to study, and a retreat can provide the time to make that wish come true. Imagine spending several hours studying the Tarot, sewing a new cloak, or inscribing a Book of Write. There is real joy in carving out this kind of devotional time, and you'll benefit in a very real way from the time spent.

Sabbatical

This approach is well known to the world of academia. In the sabbatical, the teacher steps away from the work environment for a predetermined period that may vary from a quarter of the school calendar to an entire year. The teacher retreats from the mundane, daily aspects of teaching others in order that he can find time to study, research, and teach himself. A sabbatical period is taken with specific goals in mind and is usually carefully planned and outlined. The expectation is that the intensive course of self-study, research, and practice will be returned to the classroom by the teacher/retreater with profound benefits for all. In most cases, the retreater is required to report on or in some way directly share the results of the sabbatical experience.

Stretch your retreat experience into something of a sabbatical by planning a series of smaller retreats over a period of months. If you try this, the "sabbatical" should have a single overarching goal, with each retreat meeting a smaller component of that larger goal.

Escape!

Perhaps you just want a day off to enjoy yourself—and hurrah for that! Making the time to slow down and leave the daily routine behind can be incredibly restorative. Use retreat time to read, work with your hands, engage in a magickal craft or practice, write, and so on. Giving yourself permission to devote this time to your own wants and needs may be wonderfully fulfilling, leaving you recharged and ready to face the world once again.

Thinking Forward . . .

As you begin thinking about your retreat, imagine a blank canvas on which anything might be painted. I've helped many people create retreats, and I've seen an extraordinary variety of approaches. For instance . . .

- One Pagan who was strongly aligned with the water element spent four days at the ocean, staying in a secluded beachside cabin and spending her hours wand crafting and beachcombing. She listened to the water and the wind, and she received a number of natural "messages" that buoyed her magickal inspirations—plus she was gifted with a wonderful "holey stone" talisman large enough to serve as a chalice. (Found near water, holey stones are stones that include one or more naturally occurring holes. Holey stones are felt to be particularly magickal, especially if the hole penetrates all the way through the rock.) After sitting vigil on the final night, she finished her retreat with a bonfire ritual at sunrise, dedicating her new wand and taking a new craft name that honored her connections to Mother Ocean.

- A city Witch who wanted to reconnect with her natural self spent a weekend in a tent in Arizona's mountains where she kept vigil (and watched the heavens) through the nights, greeted the sunrise each morning, slept by day, and cooked simple meals over a campfire.

- A magickal writer borrowed a friend's remote cabin, holed up there for a week, and finished a fantasy novel she'd been toying with for years. Long walks by day and nightly meditations by the fire pit fueled her efforts.

- A Druid camped in a local forest and spent the time working with the Ogham and creating his own set of Ogham sticks, something he'd always wanted to find the time for. Through this focused practice, he created a gorgeous Ogham set and discovered a previously unknown gift for divination.

- A cybermage stayed overnight in a downtown hotel—creating a fully online ritual site in "Second Life" while armed only with laptop, pizza, and endless supplies of sweetened, caffeinated soda.

- A young Wiccan finishing her solo year-and-a-day training kept vigil through the night; while "sitting by" her magickal tools she meditated on a new craft name, created her own sunrise initiation ritual, and sealed the deal by knotting a new cingulum around her waist. On the way home, she celebrated with breakfast at her favorite restaurant.

These are only a few ideas, and I hope they inspire you. Envision your own retreat as a storied landscape; your journey will take you deep within, crafting experiences limited only by your own imagination. As we work through these chapters, you'll begin imagining and creating your own specialized magickal retreat. Make note of any ideas or inspirations as they come to you—each bit of insight may play an important role in your own retreat experience.

Tasks for Chapter 2

Make notes on each of these in your retreat journal, and keep the "hero's journey" in mind as you respond.

1. Every hero's journey begins with a call. What is your "call to adventure"? What is your magickal or spiritual destiny? What do you seek?

_____

_____

_____

_____

2. What goals or needs stand unfulfilled in your life? What type of journey beckons to you?

_____

_____

_____

_____

3. What might cause you to refuse the journey? What obstacles on the "road of trials" stand between you and the retreat? For instance, you could be dealing with mundane responsibilities, the need to acquire new materials or learn new skills, the ability to get time off work, a lack of money or materials, or other factors.

_____

_____

_____

_____

4. How can you surmount these obstacles?

_____

_____

_____

_____

5. Make a list of your past and present magickal mentors. If you're self-taught, which books, online presences, or other materials have helped you learn?

_____

_____

_____

_____

6. Which of the retreat models resonate with you or excite you most at this point? Why?

_____

_____

_____

_____

Notes and Ideas:

_____

_____

_____

_____

Suggested Resources for This Chapter

Campbell, Joseph. *The Hero with a Thousand Faces.* New World Library, 2008. (*Campbell's seminal writing on the monomyth and the hero's journey.*)

Campbell, Joseph, and Bill Moyers. *The Power of Myth.* Anchor, 1991. (*Campbell's work on the importance of mythos through world cultures.*)

Jung, C. G. *The Red Book.* Norton, 2009.

Tolkien, J. R. R. *The Lord of the Rings.* London, Allen & Unwin, 1954–55.

Part II

Heeding
the Call

"Would you tell me, please, which way I ought to walk from here?" asked Alice.
"That depends a good deal on where you want to get to," said the Cat.

—LEWIS CARROLL, *ALICE'S ADVENTURES IN WONDERLAND*

Chapter Three

Who Are You,
and What Do You Need?

*Follow your bliss and the Universe will open doors for you
where there were only walls.*

—JOSEPH CAMPBELL.

Consider those times in your life that stand out as truly special or memorable. What made them that way? Simple: at those moments, you stepped outside of the routine, the mundane, and experienced something new. Think about those times . . . tally them. They're like crystalline shards lodged in one's memory, and although most are happy memories, a few are not.

For me, one of my most powerful memory-moments goes back to grade school, on the day President Kennedy was killed. Although the import was well outside of my childish understanding, I could feel the sorrow and energies swirling around me, and I knew something terrible and momentous had happened. Other memories: Seeing Glacier National Park for the first time . . . The birth of my first child . . . Receiving a Masters degree . . . The devastation of September 11, 2001 . . . The bittersweet days spent taking my children to college . . . The first time death touched me personally . . . Watching Mount St. Helens erupt . . . Seeing my first book in print . . . Working magick for the first time, and that glorious moment of knowing it was real!

Your magickal retreat will help you rediscover ways to step out of the ordinary and into the extraordinary. You'll access a special kind of intensity, creating the liminal space needed for your soul to be touched and shifting you towards meaningful personal growth. Ideally, the experience will become one of those truly memorable moments—a time in your life when you understand that something very special has happened. In other words, you will undertake and fulfill your own heroic journey, and you will be changed by the experience.

Your journey begins with questions . . .

The simplest way to start? With a self-interview:

- "If I had twenty-four hours of my own time to devote to my magickal and spiritual practices, what could I accomplish?"

Write down your responses, then continue with:

- "If I had twenty-four hours of my own to devote to my magickal and spiritual practices, what would I choose to do? How would I fill those hours?"

Take lots of notes, writing down *everything* that comes to mind, even if it may seem of little importance at the time. Allow your unconscious to speak to you—the inner voice (a.k.a., one's inner sage) is always wise. Take the inventory process further with these practical mind magicks:

Journaling

Beginning with your "what could I accomplish" and "what would I choose" answers, use your journal to expand these, capturing ideas, thoughts, and keywords. Don't miss anything: every bit of inspiration—no matter how large or small—may become a central part of your retreat experience. Take notes, make sketches, or try an invention technique. Neuroscience has shown that brainstorming types of activities are immensely useful in generating ideas; when writers are examined using positron emission tomography (PET) scanning, the brains of those using invention techniques "light up" in regions that normally sit stagnant when one simply stares at a blank piece of paper or a blank computer screen. Below are several ideas for what writing teachers call "invention"—ways of brainstorming ideas.

Freewriting

For five to ten minutes, select one of your ideas, then sit with paper and pencil and simply write whatever comes to mind. Write quickly and without thinking. Keep the pencil moving: if you can't think of something to write, doodle until you can, but keep the pencil in motion—it sounds odd, but it's an important part of the brain-to-paper process. Don't edit or censor the material, and don't worry about spelling, punctuation, or even complete sentences. Just allow the words and ideas to flow from your mind to your paper as quickly as they can.

Listing

Using a prompt or central idea, make a list of quick impressions that occur to you when you consider your idea. Try to capture sensory details: consider sounds, smells, visual elements, colors, places, and people connected to your idea.

Clustering

Write your idea in the center of a piece of paper and draw a circle around it. Think of a word that comes to mind when considering your central idea. Draw a circle around that, too, then draw a line that connects the two bubbles. Continue this process— each bubble-word can be used to generate others, and they can each be connected to other words they're related to. Continue this process until you run out of inspirations and connections. For best results, use a large piece of paper and bright or colored inks. As you might suspect, this type of invention technique works especially well for those who are visual learners.

You may want to use a "prompt" to help you begin using these techniques; some of us write more freely when given a specific idea to begin with. Here are a few prompts to help you get started:

- You're home alone, with no responsibilities and no tasks. What is the first thing you do?
- A magickal skill I've always wanted to know more about is . . .
- I have always wanted to make this magickal tool . . .

- The way I feel about the Wiccan Rede is . . .
- You carry an indigo velvet bag that holds your most special magickal materials. What's inside?
- The most magickal color is . . .
- The most important thing about the Pagan traditions is . . .
- One thing that frustrates me about my magickal path is . . .
- Open your hand to reveal a beautiful crystal.

Meditation

Meditation is a skill that takes one from a normal waking "mundane" state into a position of focused, inward calm. Through this inward focused state, meditation helps one "look in," giving a vantage and perspective that might otherwise be missed. As with journaling and invention, it's now well known that meditation allows a certain type of mental access that boosts intuition, intelligence, and memory. Recent research suggests that regular meditation relieves stress, reduces the likelihood of experiencing certain chronic illnesses, and may even extend the lifespan. Meditation is also great for gaining personal insights and retrieving memories, both of which can help you see or clarify a productive vision of the path ahead.

The balanced and/or liminal spaces provided by dawn, noon, sunset, and midnight are especially powerful times for meditation. But you can meditate at any time and in any place, provided you have the right mindset.

Before you begin, spend a few minutes thinking about your questions and ideas. If possible, choose a quiet, serene surrounding whether in- or outdoors. Center or ground and center (see the next page) before beginning.

Sit quietly in a comfortable position with your hands and arms relaxed in your lap. Either close your eyes or select a focal point to work with—a candle or crystal works well for some people. Take several long, slow, deep breaths, concentrating on feeling the air move in and out of your body. Empty your brain of all thoughts, literally thinking of nothing. Don't let your mind wander or become distracted—if you begin thinking about something, stop and whisper the words *nothing* or *clear*, then begin again to clear your mind of thoughts. Some people find it helpful to use a *mantra*, a single word that is repeated to create a near trance—e.g, *Ommmmm*.

When your meditation is finished, consciously pull your psychic self back into your human body. Centering, followed by grounding, will bring your energies back to your core, allow you to dissipate excess energy, and leave you with both restoration and a sense of completion.

Immediately after finishing your meditation, take out your journal and make notes about the experience. Meditation is an important "mind magicks" skill, and it's one that improves dramatically with practice. Journaling after each session and then reviewing your notes from time to time will provide evidence of your progress.

Grounding and Centering

Grounding

Grounding is a way to access the earth's energy and merge your own energy with it. The process anchors you to the mother planet, giving you a rock-solid foundation that is unlikely to be affected by any external energies that come your way and threaten to interrupt whatever you're doing. In addition, grounding provides a natural conduit of energy to draw into before doing any sort of energy work, and it also provides you a way to "send back" unneeded energy at the end of magick or ritual workings. Finally, it provides a powerful means of focus and a very real step between mundane and magickal realms.

To ground

Sit or stand, according to whatever feels more comfortable. Although it's possible to ground anywhere, work outdoors if you can, ideally at the base of a tree. If sitting, place your hands on the earth; if standing, reach your hands down toward the ground. Close your eyes and feel the points at which your body is touching the earth. Imagine your body growing thick roots that reach deeply into the rock and soil, becoming one with the bedrock. Visualize the roots penetrating Earth's molten core. Feel this radiant energy and imagine the energy as a single brilliant color. Taking slow, deep breaths, pull the energy and warmth up into your body, feeling the warm color and radiance surrounding you and allowing it to flood every part of your body.

Centering

Centering means taking energy and gathering it within yourself so it's focused and ready to work with. Freshly gathered energy may ping-pong around inside you, leaving you feeling edgy, unfocused, and tired; this can also lead to the "magickal hangover" that is all too common after energetic ritual work. Centering is a way to organize and focus your energy, leaving you prepared to do magick, engage in ritual, or undertake creative works.

To center

Sit quietly with eyes closed. Breathe slowly and evenly, feeling the connection between your energy and each breath. Imagine each breath pulling your energy deep into your center. For most people, the "center" is somewhere in the midsection and often right behind the navel. Feel the gathering energy as a sensation of warmth and comfort deep within.

Do I ground first? Center first? Can I center without grounding? Ground without centering?

If you feel tired or "flat," I suggest you begin with grounding. This will help you gather energy and might bring you to life a bit. Once you're "juiced up," centering will then help you organize the energies and will create a sense of focused calm.

If you feel that you're already energized but you want to create a sense of focus and readiness before you begin working, skip grounding and go directly to centering. Once centered, you'll be ready to go.

When you finish a creative or magickal activity, grounding provides a way to return excess energy back to the earth. The easiest way to do this is to ground normally, and then sit or kneel on the earth, placing your hands on the ground and sending the excess energy back through them. This is important, for leftover energy that isn't dealt with is the prime cause of the dreaded "magickal hangover," which may be characterized by nausea, agitation, fogginess, headache, and a detached feeling.

Practice grounding and centering regularly—consider them to be important parts of your magickal toolbox. Once they become familiar to you, you'll have a good sense of which one to use and when to use it.

Dreamwork

Important insights often appear through dreams, whether symbolically or literally. The meaning may not mean much at the time of the dream, but if you write down the details in a journal, the meanings may crystallize days or even months later. When using dreamwork to help you explore your own nature or needs, begin by contemplating your questions as you fall asleep. Then write your dreams down immediately after waking in the morning, before the memories dissipate. This will help you reflect on the dreams' content and meaning in the days and weeks to come.

Divination

Working with divination can be an excellent way to explore your inner thoughts and ideas, especially if you enjoy divination and are good at it. But even if divination isn't your forte, you'll find that it can speak to you in ways that may help you shape and enrich your journey.

If you like the Tarot, reach for your favorite Tarot deck. The traditional Tarot is based on the hero's journey, making it a perfect tool to use in planning the quest and trial inherent in a magickal retreat. I suggest beginning your Tarot work with a moment of centering. Shuffle the deck and hold it in your hands as you consider a central question about the goals of your retreat. Then deal the cards, creating a Tarot spread. I have two suggestions for this:

For a simple reading, use a four-card spread that summarizes the three aspects of the hero's journey: departure, initiation, and return. Prepare the cards, shuffling and cutting as desired. Cut again—this card is "you." Place it on the table so it is face up—reversals do not matter with this card. Then, deal three cards above your card—this time placing them either upright or reversed, just as dealt. The first card is about your departure, the second your initiation, and the third, your return. For a more complex reading, deal a spread with one card for each aspect of Campbell's journey metaphor, plus a card for you—the one who journeys. Use your favorite Tarot resource to interpret the meaning of the cards.

In place of (or in addition to) the Tarot, you could always try scrying with a candle flame, mirror, or crystal. Center, ask your questions, gaze into the medium, clear your mind, and see what comes. Slipping into a meditative state will make you receptive to messages and answers. If you enjoy working with runes, perhaps they will speak to you. You might choose to make a cup of tea with loose leaves and practice tasseography—the art of reading tea leaves—by looking for shapes, patterns, or messages in the residual leaves. Or, you could take a long walk, watching for natural "augurs," signs from the natural world that speak to you or seem to respond to an unanswered question.

After any divination session, make a detailed journal entry about the results. Ask yourself what you discovered, what you learned, and how this might help you develop your retreat. Write down details, and make a plan to come back and revisit your words in a month or two—you may be surprised to see how the message has unfolded since then.

Spellwork

Let's not forget the magick . . . Try creating spells or charms to inspire, deepen memory, or open your powers of intuition. You could craft a ritual for the purposes of raising energy and creativity. You might empower a talisman to carry with you throughout the retreat for mental clarity and strength of purpose. Working with your altar can be a powerful adjunct to your planning, too. Even pausing mindfully in front of the altar once or twice a day—maybe lighting a candle or whispering an incantation—will help you clear your mind and focus.

Your Inner Voice

When I was in graduate school and studying writing, one of my favorite professors would remind me that thinking was an important part of the process. Simply sitting and thinking about an idea, he pointed out, was every bit as important in the creative part of the process as was researching or creating a draft. This concept applies to your work as well. Listen to your inner voice as you contemplate and plan your retreat—it's one of your most powerful mentors. If questions or doubts come to mind, don't shuttle them aside: write them down and deal with them. This is your unconscious speaking to you in a powerful way—even if the inner voice slips into naysayer mode. Remember that the shadow is one side of the light, and vice versa. Not only do both have something to teach us, but you can't have one without the other, and it's a great truth that the most challenging times in our lives are the ones that teach us the most. If something is nagging at you, listen to it. Carefully.

On the other hand, if a specific "let's do this" idea keeps popping into your thoughts, don't ignore it either, and don't make up excuses as to why it's impractical or impossible. An idea that keeps pushing through the layers of your unconscious demands to be heard. A good seeker must be open to the message.

Goals and Goal-Setting

Now that you've developed a few ideas about how you might spend your retreat, let's try a bit of goal-setting.

Consider your magickal and/or spiritual inclinations. Let's imagine you're very interested in the Tarot and feel a strong connection to it, but you haven't had a chance to learn much about the process. Here's one possible response to these projections:

My overall goal:	I would like to develop a good basic knowledge of the Tarot, and would like to feel comfortable (and capable!) using the cards to give simple readings.
One month from now, I would like to have finished or accomplished the following:	• I will have studied each card in the major arcana. • Each day, I will draw a card from the deck and read its description in the attached guide booklet. • I'll research Tarot books and make a list of several that look promising.
Three months from now, I would like to have finished or accomplished the following:	• I will have studied each card in the minor arcana. • I'll continue a daily card draw, and will keep notes about each one so I can track how they "play out." • I will finish reading one book about the Tarot.
Six months from now, I would like to have finished or accomplished the following:	• I will explore the numerical significance and symbolism within the traditional Tarot deck. • I'll be comfortable using simple layouts to read my own cards, and will begin simple readings for a few friends or family members. • I will examine at least one additional deck. • I'll finish a second book on the Tarot.
Twelve months from now, I would like to have finished or accomplished the following:	• I will have a sound understanding of each card in the deck. • I will better understand how the Tarot works for understanding my own life. • I will be able to work with several layouts. • I'll understand the role of reversals in a reading. • I'll feel comfortable doing readings for myself and others.

Now it's your turn. What magickal interests do you have? Herbalism? Spell crafting? Working with charms or talismans? Writing? Toolcraft? Divination? Astrology? Animal pathwork? Gem and crystal magick? Astronomy? Green magick? Runes? Garb craft? Celtic studies? Archeoastronomy? Healing work? Something else?

Choose your own topic or topics and respond to the following:

My overall goal:	
One month from now, I would like to have finished or accomplished the following:	
Three months from now, I would like to have finished or accomplished the following:	
Six months from now, I would like to have finished or accomplished the following:	
Twelve months from now, I would like to have finished or accomplished the following:	

Choosing a Format for Your Retreat

In chapter 2, we explored the different kinds of retreat. Now it's time to start thinking about which one would best meet your needs. Consider the following examples:

Do I Want to . . .	Consider This Kind of Retreat . . .
Practice a skill or craft?	Try seclusion, surrounded by books and your craft materials. Build in *time* to study and practice. Gather books, tools, and materials, or arrange to include a lesson with an expert. Wallow in the experience . . .

Do I Want to …	Consider This Kind of Retreat …
Recover from a period of stress or heightened activity?	Go for the idea of sanctuary—look for a place where you can feel safe and protected, and include lots of pampering. Create a magickal spa weekend to rejuvenate and energize yourself, or head for a location with *accoutrements* and activities guaranteed to feed your soul, whether that be riding a horse along the ocean edge, soaking for hours in a hot tub, or something else. Work magicks of protection and inspiration.
Celebrate an accomplishment?	Create a secluded retreat in which you celebrate yourself. Fill the time with activities that give you pleasure. Eat delicious food. Soak in deep bathtubs. Sleep deeply. Celebrate the event by creating a lasting tool, talisman, or a piece of ritual or magickal garb.
Undertake a period of intensive study?	Aim for seclusion in a quiet, off-the-grid place—for instance, a mountain cabin or remote campsite. Support yourself with nourishing foods and bring your study materials as well as some lighter reading for the evenings. Read, take notes, repeat. Work magicks for psychic strengthening, mental clarity, and memory gifts.
Begin or end a specific project, period of training, or the like?	Create a magickal project or activity in which you demonstrate your mastery of the process. Finish with a ceremony in which you develop and put into use a personal sigil or create a new piece of regalia or a tool.

Do I Want to . . .	Consider This Kind of Retreat . . .
Undertake a self-ritual or initiation?	A vigil ceremony might be just the thing to honor your new path. Perhaps you'll watch through the night, sitting with your magickal tools and remaining open to inspirations and visitations. Create a memorable ritual, and perhaps take on a new craft name. Linger within the liminal space, then finish by setting goals for the coming year. Be aware of the rite of passage you've experienced.
Dedicate or rededicate myself to a path?	Consider some sort of vision quest, during which you prepare to receive insights to guide you along the new path. Seek a new craft name, or look for a magickal sign, talisman, or totem. Work magicks aimed at inviting a patron or deity, and gleaning wisdom from that magickal being.
Acknowledge or honor a rite of passage?	Craft a retreat that follows, as closely as possible, the hero's journey. Create a totem, tool, or piece of garb to honor your new knowledge or status. Make plans to put your new self to good use—perhaps in teaching others per the old adage "Each one, see one, do one, teach one." The student becomes the teacher . . .
Separate yourself from an unhealthy magickal setting and begin fresh with a new one?	Work with a sanctuary approach; include ritual work carefully designed to help you leave the old behind or perhaps to bridge the transition. Brush up on your protective skills: grounding and centering, shielding, warding, and banishing, as well as with low magicks designed to keep you safe—maybe creating your own poppet or hex sign.

Do I Want to . . .	Consider This Kind of Retreat . . .
Embrace the natural world?	Green magicians might benefit from a camping or backpacking trip, a day hike, a wildcrafting outing, or an entire day spent in the garden. Walk the world, watching and listening for signs and natural augury around you or for a talisman that calls your name. Finish the evening with food cooked on your own campfire—or even a roasted hot dog on a stick!
Escape?	Develop a retreat that focuses on nurturing your inner self and on just having fun! Pick those magickal tasks you enjoy most and would love to devote time to. Spend hours sinking into a fantasy novel. Hold your retreat in a soul-favorite place and feast on your favorite foods.

Meeting the Mentor

An old axiom says, "When the student is ready, the teacher will appear." The same applies to the hero's journey. Once you hear that call to destiny or adventure, and once you set foot to the path, a mentor often appears. Joseph Campbell refers to this as "supernatural aid," but mentors can be ordinary people, too.

What is a mentor? The dictionary definition describes *mentor* as "an experienced or trusted advisor" or as "someone who trains or counsels." The word comes from Latin from the ancient Greek *Mentōr*, the name of the adviser of Odysseus' young son, Telemachus, in Homer's *Odyssey*. In the *Odyssey*, note that Odysseus felt confident enough in Mentōr's skills to entrust him to much of the teaching and guardianship of his only son. Mentors have long filled positions of responsibility—and therefore, of power—in our lives. We may know mentors by a number of other names: priestess, grandfather, mother, coach, teacher, father, elder, sister, foster, and so on.

Traditional societies typically provide a shaman or elder for those going on a journey or quest, and the same is true of magickal communities that provide teachers, fosters, priestesses, or other mentors to supervise training. This guide helps the novice prepare for the experience, provides teaching, and gives her advice if she gets overwhelmed during the process. The guide may also help her evaluate the experience after it is completed, encouraging her to discover insights and formalize her learning. A guide may or may not remain available after the training is completed; note, though, that the spirit of the shared adventure is never lost.

You may be lucky enough to have a mentor available, whether through family, friends, spiritual groups, or other venues. If so, use him or her to help you plan your retreat. If you don't have a mentor at hand, try bouncing your ideas off of a magickal friend. A fresh eye will help generate new ways of looking at and evaluating any plan.

Interestingly, a magickal journal can serve as a stand-in mentor if needed. In order to make this work, you must use the journal as if you're having discussions with it. Write your observations and experiences, let the results "steep" for a few days to a week (no peeking in the meantime), then reread the material and reflect on any new perspectives that you've gained. Journal about the new results, leave them to steep once again, then return and reflect. Keep the cycle of "writing-gleaning-reflecting-asking questions-writing some more" going, allowing the journal to help you gather new insights. You'll be surprised at how useful this can be.

Let's reflect back on the ideas you've gathered in the first three chapters. Which of them could you realistically transfer into a retreat? Some of this will have to do with how much time you have available—this is something we'll explore in the next chapter. For now begin thinking about your retreat in earnest, following what I think of as the "one bite" rule. Have you heard the old riddle about how to eat an elephant? There's only one reasonable answer: "One bite at a time."

Tasks for Chapter 3

Here are a few more questions designed to help you focus your intention. The word *intend* comes from Latin roots that mean "stretch toward." In working through these tasks, you begin stretching toward your eventual retreat and preparing for the challenges and excitement you'll face in the "belly of the whale":

1. What are some of the most important things you have learned about yourself since you began studying magick?

_____

_____

_____

_____

2. What are your strengths and talents as a practitioner of magickal spirituality?

_____

_____

_____

_____

3. Where are your "weak points"—those places that would benefit by you learning more or developing additional skills?

_____

_____

_____

_____

4. What magickal subjects would you love to explore for the first time?

_____

_____

_____

_____

5. What ideas or practices might you want to explore more deeply?

_____

_____

_____

_____

6. How could you benefit from a retreat? What do you _need_?

_____

_____

_____

_____

7. What kind of a retreat are you leaning toward?

_____

_____

_____

_____

8. Practice grounding and centering daily for a period of one week. Journal each day, and at week's end, evaluate your progress.

_____

_____

_____

_____

9. Make a list of the mentors who have helped you during your magickal life. Would any of these mentors be available to work with you as you plan your retreat or continue to explore your magickal self?

_____

_____

_____

_____

Notes and Ideas

_____

_____

_____

_____

Suggested Resources for This Chapter

Allrich, Karri. *A Witch's Book of Dreams: Understanding the Power of Dreams & Symbols.* Llewellyn, 2001.

Cuhulain, Kerr. *Magickal Self-Defense: A Quantum Approach to Warding.* Llewellyn, 2008. (*An excellent book for learning core energy work and practices.*)

Gallagher, Ann-Marie. *The Spells Bible: The Definitive Guide to Charms and Enchantments.* Sterling, 2003.

Moore, Barbara. *Tarot for Beginners: A Practical Guide to Reading the Cards.* Llewellyn, 2010.

Pesznecker, Susan. *Crafting Magick with Pen and Ink: Learn to Write Stories, Spells, and Other Magickal Works.* Llewellyn, 2009.

Chapter Four

Planning Your Retreat

The beginning is the most important part of the work.

—PLATO

The Dreaded "P" Word

Planning is a word that sets some people's teeth on edge—especially many Pagans and other earth-based practitioners, who seem to have a cultural aversion to structure. This retreat is all yours, and no one is going to tell you how to put it together. But I am going to ask you to consider that a plan—even a *soft* plan—is your friend. Getting your ideas and goals down on paper will help you to be organized, and in an odd way it will also help you let go, freeing your mind from the mundane and allowing it to access the mystical. In other words, once the details are taken care of, you can set them aside and get on to the good stuff.

How you decide to plan your retreat is, of course, up to you. But in planning something this important, I encourage you to work with some kind of structure or format. Depending on your preference, this can be simple, highly detailed, or anywhere in between. Having a plan in hand will help you build and fill the hours of your retreat, and it will also guide your preparations as you organize the materials, food, and other tangible items needed. Planning also has magickal benefits as well—at least I think it does. To work with a carefully arranged set of guidelines supports intention and leaves more time for mindfulness (more on this in chapter 6).

On the other hand, while a plan will furnish structure for your retreat, it's important to retain flexibility, too. Sometimes the best things happen spontaneously, and you shouldn't be afraid to drop what you're doing and deviate from your plans if some stunning opportunity arises. This reminds me of a time when a friend and I were driving to a magickal camping gathering. Out in the middle of nowhere, we happened upon a piece of property where the owner's entire dwelling was in a series of tree houses and elevated gardens—and it was open to the public. Did we stop? You bet we did! It screwed up the schedule we'd planned for the day—and we arrived a bit late at our destination—but it was worth every second. If we'd kept driving and stuck to the plan, we'd have missed the whole thing and lost the magick as well. Instead, we deviated. And it was well worth it.

Think of it this way: a plan works like a road map for your retreat. Having a plan doesn't mean you can't take detours or follow intriguing side roads. But the road will be there, waiting for you to return to it and set to deliver you to the destination.

When Should I Retreat?

The easy answer to this is, "As soon as you can." But . . . consider that the more you think ahead and arrange at least some of the details, the more likely the experience will be both productive and wonderful.

Everyone takes a slightly different approach to this sort of planning process. Let's consider some different approaches to organizing your plans:

- Some of you will begin with **ideas**. Having begun thinking about a personal retreat, you're dazzled by the idea. You'll scan the entire book and then you'll go back and read through it, working through each step and crafting an idealized retreat experience. For you, the planning is more important than the actual time and date of the retreat. Once you've decided how much time you need and what you want to accomplish, you'll grab your calendar and set the dates.

- Some of you will begin by considering **time**. You may be bound by a tight work schedule or the needs of home and family, so your first task will be to pore over your calendar and find dates and time when a retreat will be possible. Perhaps there's a three-day weekend coming up or a vacation break in the future. Or maybe your spouse or partner is going to be out of town, leaving you a weekend ready for use. Check family and work schedules, holidays, and other existing commitments already on the calendar, then identify a retreat date and circle it in **RED** on the calendar. Hold that time as sacred and begin working toward it, fitting activities into the time available.

- Some of you may be so stressed or tired that you need the retreat to happen right now, if not sooner. For you, **need** is more important than either "ideas" or "time." You don't care so much what you do or when you do it: you just need it. If this describes you, I suggest you begin with a spontaneous mini-retreat that might fill half an hour or perhaps a couple of hours after work: perhaps a mini-rejampering (rejuvenation + pampering) "spa retreat" on a hot afternoon (see chapter 15), or a snuggle-down-and-study hour on a snowy evening, complete with hot spiced cocoa . . .

- Some of you will be pushed by **goals**. You love the idea of retreating, and you're not going to have any trouble finding time to do it, but your interest is driven by something specific you want to accomplish. This is a great way to begin, although I'll remind you that the retreat shouldn't be all business but must be fun as well.

Understand one thing: To retreat means to make time for yourself, and it's up to you to do this—no one is going to do it for you. Don't sit and wait for the "perfect" moment. Capture the inspiration, carve out the time, make the plans, and it will happen. You're doing this for *you*—make it so!

How Much Time Will I Need?

I've identified four main approaches for setting the length of a magickal retreat . . .

1. The mini-retreat: This can be anything from thirty minutes to a few hours. It can be planned, but it can also be spontaneous. I had a friend years ago who, after a particularly trying day at work, would stop at the deli, jump in her car,

and drive ninety minutes to the Pacific Ocean, where she'd eat her sandwich on the beach and watch the sunset. She did this a few times each year and it fed her soul and eased her frustrations, leaving her ready to return to the city and the "real world." Apply this idea to your own life and you'll find that even a lunch hour or other small chunk of time can provide an opportunity for a mini-retreat and might be just what you need. It's definitely not as beneficial as a full-length retreat experience, but it's a great start.

2. <u>Daylong retreat</u>: This retreat begins and ends on the same day. Although this doesn't allow the time and feel of an overnight retreat, you can still accomplish quite a lot in several hours, and it's long enough to give you a sense of the luxurious feeling embedded in a longer retreat. This time frame works well for personal study, craft projects, or other goal-specific work.

3. <u>Overnight retreat</u>: This retreat includes at least one overnight period, whether for sleep, vigil, stargazing, fire circle, ritual, or any number of nocturnal activities. The overnighter is a great way to retreat as it allows access to liminal times of day—sunset, twilight, midnight, dawn, sunrise—as well as providing opportunities for just about any sort of magickal work, including vigil and vision quest. The weekend is an easy time for most people to accomplish an overnighter, but consider, also, that a mid-week retreat is often extra quiet (everyone else is at work) and is a wonderful goal if you can manage it.

4. <u>Long-length retreat</u>: This one includes at least two overnight periods and can be as long as you care to make it. The long retreat does it all—it gives you time to do whatever you want and also provides a way to touch or bring in magick from any part of the day or night. A really long retreat of several days to a week is ideal if you can manage it, as the length allows maximum benefit from the feeling of being separated from "real time." The time span also provides time to accomplish just about any reasonable goal, as well as making it more likely that you'll have that wonderful feeling of entering actual magickal "other space." Note, too, that a long retreat time makes it possible for you to travel some distance to and from the retreat site—allowing you access to camping spots, fabulous bed and breakfasts, national parks, or other retreat-worthy locations.

Whichever form you select, aim for as much uninterrupted, quiet time as possible. You're retreating—the idea is to find haven and solitude and a place to hunker down and listen to whatever voices are clamoring to be heard.

Setting and Place

All of us have special places in which we feel peaceful and serene—often, these places are linked to the place where we spent our childhoods, but we can find them in other sites as well. For me, the best place on Earth is the Columbia River Gorge. I have only to drive or walk into the Gorge to feel like I'm home; cares drop away and time seems to slow down. I always return home feeling rested and calm from feeling the presence of the trees, mountains, and river and from breathing the clear, sweet air, even if only for a couple of hours. If you have a favorite setting like this one, it can provide a spectacular getaway.

Some people prefer to retreat in comfortable indoor settings, while others think the only way to have the experience is in the outdoors. Spend time thinking about your own choice. Where are your favorite places that are reasonably close by? What places inspire you? Which ones make you feel safe, protected, or well rested? Meditate on the question, imagining yourself on a personal journey. What do the surroundings look like?

For best results, I strongly advise you to seek out a location away from your daily surroundings, as this helps one feel the movement into "other space" that should accompany a good retreat. However, some people may have to retreat at home, and your own home may work, especially if you live alone. If retreating at home, you'll have to plan carefully to make sure that you have the time and space to carry out the experience and meet all of your goals. Even more, you'll need to work hard to create a sense of being "somewhere else," which means you'll need to cloak the familiar in some way, as well as avoiding distraction by the routine and mundane. Keep reminding yourself that your retreat, in order to be most effective, must transport you into someplace that is *different*.

If you're really lucky, you may have access to a cabin in the woods, a beach house, or some other kind of vacation property. Be creative in discovering what's available in your area. Here in the Pacific Northwest, you could arrange to stay in a beach cabin, a yurt, a submarine, a forest service lookout tower, a houseboat, a Native American lodge (a.k.a. tipi), or a lighthouse, to name some of the more interesting getaways. A truly unique location may add a fascinating angle to your retreat. You might also consider an interesting hotel or a bed and breakfast. Or maybe you have a friend who'd entertain a house-swap.

If the weather is fair, you could arrange a camping getaway. You could even decide to "camp" in your back yard. A daylong retreat could focus on a long out-and-back hike with a picnic lunch and magickal work to do en route. Do you live near any national parks? They're some of the most magickal places on Earth and guaranteed to provide an ethereal focus for your work. Many state and regional parks are also spectacular and allow camping, lodging, and/or day use.

Wherever you end up, be sure you've paid attention to paperwork, payments, reservations, and permissions. Yes, the red tape can be annoying, but it's even more annoying to have your experience disrupted because you forgot to manage the details or because you find you're in violation of one law or another. Bummer.

Timing

You'll want to consider timing details when planning your retreat and your activities. For instance, consider the power of a vigil planned on a full or dark moon, at the time of an eclipse, or on one of the eight Sabbats. Is there a season you prefer or a specific holiday or date you would like to observe or include? What about a retreat that coincides with a meteor shower, the return of the whales, or the coloring of the fall leaves? Correspondences linked with day, season, month, moon phase, and natural events may have profound effects on your retreat magicks and on the outcome.

Time of Day

Consider the time when your retreat will begin, reach its high point, and end; working with the time of day is a powerful way to empower your plans.

- <u>Dawn</u> is the time of day when we see the first light in the sky but without the sun yet visible. Dawn is a threshold point, marking the change from night to day. This is a powerful liminal time and a good time to celebrate births, to conclude initiations or vigils, or to mark any type of transformation.

- <u>Sunrise</u> takes place when the sun appears over the horizon, filling the world with a renewed spark of light and the promise of warmth. It's the perfect time to begin a retreat, to conclude a vigil, or to work magick for new beginnings or initiations. Sunrise and sunset mirror the give-and-take between light and dark; they're excellent times to do spirit work, penetrate the veil between the worlds, or seek out the wee folk.

- During the <u>morning</u> hours, the sun's energy grows, and warmth and light wash over the world. Visibility and clarity are the words of the hour. It's a powerful time for anything involving creativity, like writing, garb- or toolcraft, or candle magicks. Morning is a great choice for physical activities, such as walking, yoga, or healing work, as the morning hours are in synch with upswings in our bodies' hormone and catecholamine levels. It's often the best time of day to harvest and work with herbs and to observe birds and animals.

- <u>Noon</u>, in my tradition, is a time of balance, with the sun directly overhead and its radiance and power at a peak. Choose the noon hour for work with solar or male energies as well as with any practices involving balance, reflection, or other mirroring skills. It's an ideal time to work with divination, given that the sun's pull is relatively even, constant, and balanced ("poised" overhead). Noon is also a sound time for developing plans that are even-handed and free from bias. Note that some practitioners view noon more as a time of tension or power rather than balance; in this case, consider working with the ideas of maximum heat and maximum power that follow the sun's movements and position at noon.

- During the <u>afternoon</u>, the sun's light energy begins to ebb as the sun moves toward sunset. Work with waning energies is well done during the afternoon. However, even as the light wanes, the sun's energies have heated the Earth, which usually means that the day's hottest temperatures happen in the afternoon. This may feed into your intentions, and is a great time for outdoor activities. On the other hand, if the weather is simply too hot, an afternoon siesta may be a better choice. Once the sun begins ebbing, lunar energies begin rising. This transitional time of day provides opportunity for quiet study and reading and is excellent for all kinds of nature studies.

- <u>Sunset</u> takes place when the sun moves below the horizon, returning the world to shadow and then darkness. Mirroring sunrise, it's a good time to conclude a retreat or begin a vigil as well as to do work with spirit folk or the veil between the worlds. Sunset represents a time of "potential," as the energies of day switch to those of night. Sunset is also quite beautiful.

- Dusk (also called twilight) refers to that time after the sun has set but during which light still lingers in the sky. Like dawn, it's a threshold point of transition, and it's also a time of great power as the sun's energies ebb and give way to those of the moon. This is a good time to do work that reaches into other planes or dimensions, or that attempts to contact other beings. Astral travel and healing by distance are well done at this time, as are magicks dealing with transformation or metamorphosis.

- Night refers to the dark nighttime hours, during which there is no appreciable sunlight. Since vision is less available, one must rely on sound, touch, and smell. Temperature falls, too, and life seems to slow down. Night is a perfect time to explore mysteries or consider the unknown. It's a good time for some types of divination and meditation as well, and the entire nighttime span is *the* time for stargazing and working with the cosmos.

- Midnight: Like noon, this is another time of balance, with the sun at its greatest ebb and the heavenly bodies at their maximum power. Midnight is often called "the witching hour." In those traditions that honor the moon as "female," this is the time to work spells requiring a female correspondence or honoring a female deity. The night's darkest skies happen between midnight and late night, providing optimum conditions for stargazing. Note: As with the discussion of "noon," above, if you regard midnight in some way other than a time of balance, please adjust your practices accordingly.

- The late night or "wee hours" are night personified. These are times of deep darkness and high magicks. Everything is cloaked by the absence of lights, and anything can happen. Late night is prime time for vigils and vision quests with the mind left open to spirit visitations. Night itself becomes a kind of liminal space and provides a chance for seekers to stand in many places at once.

Day of Week

You may wish to consider how daily influences can dovetail with your intentions. Starting or ending your retreat on a specific day—or using a certain day to carry out specific parts of your retreat—may reap powerful results.

- <u>Monday</u> is the "Moon's Day," and a good time for magick with a feminine or "new birth" aspect as well as beginnings or initiations. A retreat begun or focused on Monday would also be an auspicious time for retreats aimed at self-nurturing or self-empowering. If you're working with the moon, you won't find a better day than Monday.

- <u>Tuesday</u> is "Tyr's (or Tiw's) Day." This day is under the rule of Mars and is ideal for spells involving strength, courage, and power. Is there a challenge you'd like to take on? Tuesday might be the ideal day to do it.

- <u>Wednesday</u> is "Woden's Day" (a.k.a. Odin's Day). Ruled by Mercury, Wednesday is an apt time for work involving wisdom, creativity, and divination. If your retreat will include study and practice, Wednesday would make a great focus.

- <u>Thursday</u> is "Thor's Day." Ruled by Jupiter, Thursday provides a sound opportunity for magick focusing on money, luck, and success. If you plan to do works focusing on future success or fruition, Thursday would be a great choice.

- <u>Friday</u> is "Freya's Day," ruled by Venus. Spells and magickal works for love, romance, friendship, and beauty are well done on Friday. Will your retreat focus on you or on relationships? Don't overlook Friday.

- <u>Saturday</u> is "Saturn's Day," and is ruled by the planet Saturn. Work magick for protection, structure, separation, and resolution on Saturday. There's no better time to conduct banishings, wardings, protective spells, cord magicks, severings, and the like.

- <u>Sunday</u> is the "Sun's Day." Ruled by the sun, this is an optimal day for masculine magick and workings involving peace, harmony, health, strength, and divine power. Obviously, it's also a fabulous time to work with any type of solar deities or energies.

The Seasons, Months, and Sabbats

Like the days of the week, seasons and months have their own magickal traditions and correspondences, and if you plan your retreat far enough ahead, you may be able to select a season and perhaps a month that perfectly suit your purposes. Even if you can't plan this far out, you can certainly study and use these attributes to enhance your experience.

The Sabbats—traditionally pronounced suh-BOTs—are eight seasonal markers spaced evenly throughout the Gregorian year. Widely regarded as sacred, the Sabbats are celebrated differently by different traditions, but a deep respect for the earth and the inevitable turning of life's seasonal, cyclical wheel is always at the center.

Four of the Sabbats fall on the four solstices and equinoxes and are known as "quarter days," while those between the quarter days—Samhain, Imbolc, Beltaine, and Lughnasadh—are called "cross-quarter days." If your retreat will happen during one of the Sabbats, making that celebration part of your focus could reap wonderful results.

Winter

Winter is a time of symbolic "death." But it really isn't death—it's a time of sleep and repose, a time when energies wind down and the natural world rests and gathers energy. A winter retreat is an ideal time for planning and contemplation or for any sort of quiet activity. Tools crafted during winter will be full of sequestered power and intention. Winter is also a powerful time for intuition and for intuitive activities, like writing, and it also works well with magicks aimed at banishing or severing—i.e., work with the Dark Arts.

December

December comes from a Latin root meaning "ten" and was the tenth month of the Roman year. December marks the beginning of winter with the astronomical **winter solstice**—the longest night of the year—falling on the 21st or 22nd. The sun reaches its lowest position above the horizon, resulting in long, dark nights and short, dim days as the great seasonal wheel reaches a turning point and rotates toward the light. During this time, Earth awakens from sleep and days begin to lengthen and temperatures to slowly rise. It's not surprising that ancient peoples rejoiced at the winter solstice, for they knew that warmth, light, and abundant food would soon come again.

Many magickal folks celebrate this solstice as the Sabbat of **Yule**. Yule marks the year's shortest day and longest night and honors the returning light and life that will lead inexorably to springtime. Symbols of lights, evergreens, and feasting are an important part of Yule. From a retreat perspective, Yule is an excellent time to study, create tools, or conceive plans.

January

January is deep winter. The light is returning, but the cold, in most locations, has reached its depths and this is when most places experience their most severe winter weather. For those who follow a Gregorian calendar, January 1 marks the beginning of the New Year. The word *January* comes from the god Janus, who had two or three faces and could look both forward and backward in time. Janus was the god of gateways and ruled over beginnings and ends, past and future. Janus's head is always shown with two or three separate gazes and faces; this multidirectional gaze symbolizes vigilance and new beginnings, reminding people to continually be aware of what surrounds them and of the peril that results when they lose sight of their path.

The first weeks of January are ruled by the zodiacal sign of Capricorn, which is all about honor, duty, and perseverance. Late in January, the zodiac swings forward and enters Aquarius, a sign associated with friendship, ideals, and creativity. January is a great time for retreats focusing on creative projects, toolcraft, and other hands-on activities.

February

February typically is characterized by slightly warmer temperatures and possibly, depending on where you live, the first signs of spring. There is a strong sense of emerging from sleep, stretching one's arms, and preparing for action. The word *February* comes from the Middle English *feverer*, from Old French *feverier*, based on Latin *Februarius*, from *februa*, the name of a purification feast held during the month. February begins under the zodiacal sign of Aquarius and moves into Pisces, the place of dreams and imagination.

Imbolc

Imbolc (EE-melk) falls on February 1–2, and this cross-quarter Sabbat honors the earliest signs of spring. In Celtic traditions, it's synonymous with spring lambings, the births of baby animals, and the filling of mothers' breasts with milk. If you want to work with ideas of "fresh starts" or beginning a new path or process, this is a most opportune time to do so. It's also a lovely time for a "spa" retreat as we move from winter's depths into the promise of the coming spring.

Spring

Spring is the time of awakenings, fresh growth, and new beginnings. This is the perfect time to work with initiations or to put new projects, plans, or goals into movement.

March

March features the **spring equinox**, the official welcome to the spring season. At the time of the equinox, the sun's ecliptic rotational pattern crosses the celestial equator, resulting in day and night that are both about twelve hours long. It's a time of celestial balance and poise. The month's name harkens back to Middle English, from an Old French dialect variant of *marz*, from Latin *Martius*, "month of Mars." March begins in Pisces but transitions into the zodiacal sign of Aries, associated with Mars-like passion, fiery temperament, and courageous actions.

The spring equinox takes place on or around March 20 and is often called **Ostara** (oh-STAR-uh) or **Eostre** (ee-OH-stir). This Sabbat honors the earnest beginning of spring, and its most common symbolic manifestation is via the egg, which is the seed or beginning of all things. Fresh grasses, early greens and herbs, and young animals are other signs of Ostara. The spring equinox is an excellent time for retreats devoted to initiations, beginnings, or setting plans in motion. It's also a powerful time simply to honor life in all its guises.

April

April is early spring. Morning frosts have stopped in many climates, and plants and trees burst with leaf and bud. New seeds and trees are tucked into the earth with hopes of summer bounty and fall harvest. The month's name comes from Old English, derived from the Latin *Aprilis*, which shares a root with the name Aphrodite. April is, indeed, a time of freshness and astounding, simple beauty. Toward the end of April, the zodiac takes us out of Aries and into Taurus, a sign of calm and contentment (and a nice antidote to the energy of Aries!). This is a good time for retreats devoted to ritual work or the practice of magickal skills.

May

May is high spring in its element. The month kicks off with the cross-quarter Sabbat of Beltaine, a time for celebrating the fertility and fecundity of the season as life of all kinds bursts forth from Earth's collective wombs. The month's name comes from late Old English, from Old French *mai*, from Latin *Maius (mensis)*, meaning "(month) of the goddess Maia." Links to the fertility cycle and the menses are clear. May begins in Taurus and then moves into Gemini, a sign associated with curiosity, a quick wit, and an urge to explore.

Beltaine

The Sabbat of **Beltaine** (traditionally BEE-ell-TIN-yuh, although most magickal folks simply say BELL-tain.) falls on May 1 and is synonymous with fertility and fecundity. Beltaine is regarded as a joyful, passionate time and is excellent for fire circles, physical activity, sex magick, and impassioned works of all kinds. It's also the traditional time for dancing and for circling the maypole, an ancient phallic symbol of regeneration. Express creativity and do emotional work at Beltaine.

Summer

Summer is the time of fruition and bounty during which we see the full results of plans put into practice months earlier. This is a particularly auspicious time to make anything that you wish to fill with power, whether that be a magickal tool, a piece of garb, or a Book of Shadows. It's also prime time for working with energy and strength.

June

June hosts the **summer solstice,** which falls on or around the 21st. Ironically, while most in the northern hemisphere see June as the beginning of summer, the solstice marks the longest day of the year, after which sunlight diminishes a little bit more each day. June brings, however, a promise of warm temperatures and all of summer's joyful bounty. The month's name is from Middle English, from Old French *juin*, from Latin *Juniu*, "sacred to Juno," a Roman state goddess. With the summer solstice, the zodiac moves from Gemini and into Cancer, ushering in a period of imagination and creativity. This is an opportune time for retreats focusing on arts, crafts, hearth skills, and the like.

Many magickal folks celebrate the summer solstice as the Sabbat called **Litha** (LEE-thuh). It's the opposite of the winter solstice, marking the longest day and shortest night of the year. Rather ironically, although the summer solstice actually portends the return of darkness—with shortening days from then until the winter solstice—most people view this June Sabbat as the onset of summer. Whatever the view, it is a time to celebrate joy, positivity, and potential. The traditional symbols are related to the sun: sunflowers, fresh foods, flowers, and anything brilliant yellow.

July

July finds summer solidly underway. With the sun high in the sky and overhead for several hours each day, both day and night temperatures are pleasant and warm. Named for Julius Caesar, July is tailor-made for enjoyment and celebration, making it a perfect time for beach trips, barbecues, stargazing, camping, bike rides, and the other joys of a summer outdoors. It's also a perfect time for outdoor retreats. July begins in the zodiacal sign of Cancer and moves into Leo, launching opportunities for hard work and generosity.

August

August is high summer. Springing from the mid-seventeenth-century French *auguste* and the Latin *augustus*, "consecrated, venerable," August is a month worshipped by many as a carefree time of vacations, barbecues, and lemonade, as well as the time when gardens and farms begin pouring out their bounties. That which was planned in winter and planted in spring finds its yield now, in high summer. At the end of August, the zodiacal movement takes us out of Leo and into Virgo. Virgo is known for inspiring organization and tenacity, and it's a superb time for deep study and exploration.

Many Pagans and other magickal folks honor the August 1 Sabbat of **Lughnasadh** (traditionally LOO-nuss-ah), also called **Lammas** (LOM-uss) by many. The word *Lammas* means "loaf mass," and Lughnasadh is, indeed, a celebration of the grain harvest and of other fresh growing foods, particularly regional berries. Use this Sabbat to honor Earth and her sustainability; a green magick-based retreat would work fabulously in August. This is also a great time to reflect on plans that have been successful, resulting in one's own sustainable "harvest."

Autumn (Fall)

Autumn is harvest time. We gather our bounty, storing it carefully for future sustenance and giving thanks for the good that has come to us over the past year. Autumn reminds us to plan ahead and prepare thoughtfully for whatever's coming down the road.

September

September is from the Latin *septem*, "seven," the seventh month of the Roman year. September is harvest epitomized as we bring in the fruits of summer and prepare for the coming winter. The nights are beginning to chill; the leaves are starting to turn; and early frosts may occur; but September is still glorious. The **fall (autumnal) equinox** falls on or around September 20. Like the spring equinox, the fall equinox is a time of balance and equanimity, as well as a time to celebrate and "bring in" the harvest. During September, the zodiac turns from Virgo and moves into Libra, creating an atmosphere of harmony, peace, and diplomacy.

Many celebrate the fall equinox as the Sabbat **Mabon** (MAY-bonn), which marks the end of summer and the coming of autumn. Mabon is a harvest celebration, and focuses on symbols of harvest, sustenance, and plenty. It also provides a comment on careful planning, for only if we care sensibly for the harvest will we make it through the dark, cold period of winter. A retreat in September might work with change and transformation as the world spins toward winter.

October

October is autumn's knife edge, as summer fully ebbs and we prepare for winter's "little death." Named for *octo*, "eight," October was the eighth month of the Roman calendar. For those who practice earth-based traditions, October is full-on autumn, with leaves dropped or dropping and nights sinking into dark chill. During this time of transition, spirits and gates into the spirit world abound. In late October, the zodiac leaves Libra and enters Scorpio, a time of both intensity and mystery.

Most Pagans celebrate the Sabbat of **Samhain** (traditionally SAW-win or SOW-inn) on October 31. For all who follow earth-based traditions, Samhain is an important high holy day; for those who follow Celtic or Druid practices, Samhain marks the New Year. The veil between the worlds is thin at Samhain, making it an excellent time to honor or commune with the departed or with deities, as well as working with any form of divination or ritual magick.

November

November's name comes from the Latin *novum*, "nine," showing its place as the ninth month of the Roman calendar. November is dark, cold, and sometimes stormy, with occasional last gasps of brilliant sun. For many, November finds us beginning preparations for winter celebrations, including a keen awareness that winter will soon arrive and, with it, the cycle of darkness will again swing toward light. Toward the end of November, the zodiac takes us out of Scorpio and moves into Sagittarius. It's a good time to focus on pathwork or psychic arts.

And the Great Wheel turns anew . . .

The Sun and Moon

In symbolic terms, the sun is said to rule the day, while the moon rules the night. The sun's power begins with dawn, emerges at sunrise, waxes through the morning, peaks at noon, fades through the afternoon, and finishes at sunset. In contrast, the moon's power begins in the late afternoon, emerges at sunset, waxes through the evening, peaks at midnight, fades through the late night hours, and finishes at sunrise. Note that these are the traditional "times" for solar and lunar powers; there will be differences, depending on seasons and on the lunar cycles. For instance, even though we can see certain moon phases during daylight, most people still count this time as belonging to the sun. Likewise, when summer nights grow long and the sun lingers into the evening hours we associate with night, most still associate the evening hours as ruled by the moon.

Energy is also governed by the lunar phases. The moon orbits Earth, and the changing relationships between Earth and moon create changes in how fully the moon is lit up by the sun—we see these changing relationships as lunar phases. The period between the new (dark) moon and full moon is the waxing (growing) phase and is associated with magicks involving growth, empowerment, beginnings, initiations, and the like. The opposite period—between full and new moon—is the waning (diminishing) phase and corresponds with energy gathering, winding down, or binding types of magicks, as well as with conclusions and endings. The entire lunar cycle has eight sections, making the number eight sacred to the moon: new, waxing crescent, waxing half, waxing gibbous, full, waning gibbous, waning half, and waning crescent.

Celestial alignments may create eclipses at the time of the full or new moon. When the earth is directly between the sun and moon, our planet's shadow is cast over the moon and a lunar eclipse occurs. When the moon passes between the sun and Earth, the moon's shadow is cast over the sun and a solar eclipse occurs. Eclipses may be total or partial, depending on how the celestial bodies align. A good resource for eclipses is the *Old Farmer's Almanac*, which lists them for the entire coming year. You'll also find a number of good astronomy websites that list eclipses—with their times and viewing locations—for years to come.

Both solar and lunar eclipses are times of potent magicks and mysteries, especially when dust in Earth's atmosphere makes the eclipsed moon appear blood red, or when the "diamond ring" appears around the eclipsed sun. Imagine what early humans must have thought as they watched the sun or moon disappear, uncertain if it would ever return. If you can incorporate an eclipse time into your retreat, know that you will be working with some extraordinary magicks.

An important safety note: Never look directly at the sun or at the eclipsed sun; permanent retinal burning and damage may result. Of course, don't look directly at the sun through binoculars or a telescope either, as the potential damage is further magnified. If you have a chance to view a solar eclipse, create a pinhole camera or shop for a pair of sun-safe viewing lenses. A quick surf of the Internet will help you find these items.

The Esbats

The Esbats (ESS-bots or EZ-botts) are periods of ritual or celebration held at the full moons. The origin of the word *Esbat* is unknown; some claim that it may come from the Old French *s'esbattre*, which is loosely translated as "frolic joyfully."

The moon, our closest celestial body and one that is visible in our night sky for half the nights of each month, has always been a focus of magick and wonder, and it seems obvious that people would work magick and dance in the moonlight. Rituals carried out under the full moon will abound in power and energy—indeed, the lunar energies can be "drawn down" in ritual work and used to empower tools, workings, ritual, or even ourselves.

Aboriginal peoples and different cultures have long made a practice of assigning names to the full moons, and because of this, most full moon names clearly follow what we think of as seasonal or agricultural calendars. Several of these are below;

perhaps one or more will flip a switch or inspire you as you think about your retreat. Note that uses may vary according to regional and geographic traditions:

- **January:** Cold Moon, First Moon, Ice Moon, Moon After Yule, Old Moon, Snow Moon, Storm Moon, Winter Moon, Wolf Moon
- **February:** Budding Moon, Chaste Moon, Famine Moon, Hunger Moon, Opening Buds Moon, Trapper's Moon
- **March:** Crow Moon, Crust Moon, Fish Moon, Frog Moon, Lenten Moon, Maple Sugar Moon, Sap Moon, Sleeping Moon, Windy Moon
- **April:** Awakening Moon, Egg Moon, Fish Moon, Flower Moon, Frog Moon, Grass Moon, Growing Moon, Peony Moon, Pink Moon, Seed Moon, Sprouting Grass Moon, Wildcat Moon
- **May:** Budding Moon, Corn Moon, Corn Planting Moon, Dragon Moon, Dyad Moon, Flower Moon, Hare Moon, Milk Moon, Planting Moon
- **June:** Lotus Moon, Mead Moon, Rose Moon, Strawberry Moon, Windy Moon, Wort Moon
- **July:** Blood Moon, Buck Moon, Crane Moon, Dyad Moon, Hay Moon, Hungry Ghost Moon, Summer Moon, Thunder Moon
- **August:** Barley Moon, Dog Day's Moon, Fruit Moon, Grain Moon, Lightning Moon, Red Moon, Ripe Corn Moon, Sturgeon Moon, Women's Moon
- **September:** Barley Moon, Chrysanthemum Moon, Harvest Moon, Moon of Pairing, Nut Moon, Singing Moon
- **October:** Blackberry Moon, Blood Moon, Early Snow Moon, Gourd Moon, Hunter's Moon, Kind Moon, Falling Leaves Moon
- **November:** Beaver Moon, Dark Moon, Frost Moon, Oak Moon, Trading Moon, White Moon
- **December:** Bitter Moon, Long Nights Moon, Moon Before Yule, Twelfth Moon

As you read through these, it's easy to visualize the ways our ancestors tracked the seasonal changes in the world around them. Work with these ideas to capture some of these energies in your own full moon retreat. You might even consider creating your own full moon name to mark the occasion: e.g., "Initiation Moon," "Moon of Learning," "Vigil Moon," "Retreat Moon," "Quest Moon," or something similar.

Astrological Influences

Astrology is the practice of interpreting the positions of heavenly bodies and divining their influences on human lives. It dates back to at least 2500 BCE and was part of the practices of the ancient Sumerians, among others. People today use astrology to understand their own natures as well as to consider the past, present, and future. If you work with astrology, you may be interested in timing your retreat in terms of astrological positions, or you could use your retreat time to study astrology or work with your own birth chart.

To delve into an explanation of astrology is beyond the course of this book—indeed, it would take an entire book even to begin to explore the subject. Go back to the previous section on seasons, and you'll find a quick mention of the zodiacal signs in terms of the months. Otherwise, if astrology is important to your practices, and if you plan to include astrology in your retreat, you should use your resources to incorporate these ideas into your plan.

Planetary Hours

The system of planetary hours assigns each hour of the twenty-four-hour cycle to a specific celestial body: sun, moon, and the non-Earth visible planets—Mercury, Venus, Mars, Jupiter, and Saturn. The standard magickal reference is Peter of Abano's "Table of the Planetary Hours," which is easy to find on the Internet (and is listed at the end of this chapter and in Appendix A). Your retreat activities may be enhanced when timed to coincide with a correspondence-matched planetary hour.

The Night Sky

Use an astronomy website, the latest *Old Farmer's Almanac*, or a copy of the annual *We'Moon* to find out which planets or astronomical events will be flying by or circling overhead when you retreat. Constellations, comets, meteor showers, visible planets, planetary conjunctions, eclipses, and other celestial spectacles lend magick to your retreat and might even give you a specific focus.

Important Dates

What calendar dates are important to you? Think about birthdays, anniversaries, the start of your year-and-a-day training, or the conclusion of fostership. If appropriate and meaningful, look for ways to work these special days into your retreat, either as a focus or as a way to enrich the experience.

Numbers and Numerology

Dates can be reduced using a simple form of numerology. Many of us magick-users have an affinity with one or more numbers, and each of the ordinary numbers one through ten has its own specific attributes:

- One (from old Latin and the Greek *Monad)*: Purity, unity, and focus
- Two (*Dyad*): Polarity, duality, and balance
- Three (*Triad*): Strength, stability, tension, God/dess focus, and Druid magicks
- Four (*Tetrad*): Foundation, the elements (earth-air-fire-water), and Earth
- Five (*Pentad*): The fifth element (spirit), the magickal realm, Wicca, Paganism, light, health, and vitality
- Six (*Hexad*): Perfection, creation, and the universe
- Seven (*Heptad*): Spirituality, spiritual wholeness, sacred magicks, and mysteries
- Eight (*Octad*): Natural magicks, ethical practices, infinity, visible planets, and lunar magicks. Astronomers who photograph the moon's position in the sky over time find that she traces an analemma: a combination between a figure eight and the infinity symbol. The path to Buddhist enlightenment also has eight steps.
- Nine (*Ennead*): Magick, Witches' magicks, perfection, and the idea of a limitless scope
- Ten (*Decad*): Completion, realization, and perfection

Note that each letter of the alphabet also has a numerical association, meaning that words can also be reduced in numerological terms.

If a specific number is very important to you, you might consider simple numerology when planning your retreat date. For instance, let's imagine you had a choice of beginning your retreat on June 7, 2012 or June 23, 2012.

June 7, 2012 = 6 (June is the sixth month) + 7 + 2 + 1 + 2 = 18
18 = 1 + 8 = **9**

June 23, 2012 = 6 + 2 + 3 + 2 + 1 + 2 = 16
16 = 1 + 6 = **7**

If you favored the number seven, and particularly if your retreat was going to have a specifically spiritual focus, it might be more auspicious to begin your retreat on June 23 than on June 7 in order to benefit from correspondences associated with seven. On the other hand, if you followed a Wiccan path and planned to do ritual as part of a retreat, planning so that the final night fell on June 7 would correspond with the magick of nine, and would help create a powerful ending to the experience.

Family, Pets, and Others

When helping others plan a retreat, I often hear questions like, "What about my dog?" or "Can I take my partner/husband/child?"

The simplest answer is "No." Think again about why you're doing the retreat: this experience is all about you and your personal growth. In order for this to be a rich experience of growth or rejuvenation, you must be able to devote the time to yourself without any distractions. You need to put yourself first for this short period, and you should feel free to be rather selfish about this. Time and privacy in today's uber-digital 24/7 world are precious commodities, and you must guard them well, for your personal well-being is at stake. And let's face it: no matter how much you love your husband, no matter how sure you are that no one but you can take proper care of your child, no matter that your dog or cat is your familiar . . . if any of them come with you on your retreat, you'll be distracted and lose focus, and the retreat will no longer be about you.

Your task on retreat is to step into liminal space and come face to face with your own magickal self in hopes of achieving personal growth and insights. You can't do this when you're distracted by or paying attention to someone else, whether human or animal. Once again, I encourage you to leave them at home. Devote time to your own spiritual renewal, and your loved ones will not only welcome you home but will also benefit through your experience.

Group Retreats

As I mentioned earlier in this book, there may be times when a group—a coven, for instance—wants to retreat together to accomplish some sort of magickal goal or purpose. I devote a special chapter to this later in the book, but understand that the same planning components apply, whether for individual or group purpose. Most important of all: everyone in the group must share a common goal and vision in order for a group retreat to be successful, and each individual must be prepared to set aside his or her own "wants" in order to focus energy on the group goal. In an individual retreat, the focus is on <u>one</u> person, while in a group retreat, it's all about the group.

Tasks for Chapter 4

Planning the details of your retreat finds you taking your first step along "the road of trials." In your journal, record responses to the following prompts.

1. Where are your special places, and how close can you come to them?

  _____

  _____

  _____

  _____

2. Suggest at least two possible dates for your retreat.

  _____

  _____

  _____

  _____

3. Suggest one or two tentative places for your retreat.

_____

_____

_____

_____

4. Choose a time format: will you do a mini-, daylong, overnight, or long-length retreat?

_____

_____

_____

_____

5. List or discuss how (or if) you'll consider the following in planning your retreat:

   • Time of day

   • Day of week

   • Months

   • Seasons

   • Sabbats

   • Esbats

   • Sun and moon

- Astrological influences

- Planetary hours

- The night sky

- Numbers and dates

6. Have you accepted the call to adventure? Explain.

_____

_____

_____

_____

Notes and Ideas

_____

_____

_____

_____

Suggested Resources for This Chapter

Abano, Peter of. "The Initial Rites and Ceremonies." Sacred-Texts.com. (n.d.) Online at http://www.sacred-texts.com/grim/bcm/bcm42.htm. (*Includes the tables of planetary hours.*)

Conway, D. J. *Moon Magick: Myth & Magic, Crafts & Recipes, Rituals & Spells.* Llewellyn, 2002.

Gallagher, Ann-Marie. *The Wicca Bible: The Definitive Guide to Magic and the Craft.* Sterling, 2005.

George, Demetra, and Douglas Birch. *Astrology for Yourself: How to Understand and Interpret Your Own Birth Chart.* Ibis, 2006. (*An excellent introductory text for those new to astrology, but detailed enough for the experienced user as well.*)

Illes, Judika. *Element Encyclopedia of Witchcraft.* Thorsons, 2005. (*An encyclopedic work by Illes; this one focuses on different elements of craft, correspondences, etc.*)

———. *Encyclopedia of 5000 Spells.* HarperOne, 2009. (*Another encyclopedic tome of spellcraft, components, and so much more.*)

Lippincott, Kristen. *Astronomy (DK Eyewitness Books).* DK Children, 2008. (*An image-rich guide that provides a wonderful introduction to astronomy.*)

The Old Farmer's Almanac. Old Farmer's Almanac, published annually.

We'Moon: Gaia Rhythms for Womyn. Mother Tongue Ink, 2011. (*Published continually since 1980, this annual combines a datebook format with art, poetry, readings, moon lore, and astrology. Although decidedly woman-centered, it is full of wonderful magick and interpersonal insights that anyone could use.*)

Zell-Ravenheart, Oberon. *Companion for the Apprentice Wizard.* New Page Books, 2004. (*A detail-packed sequel to Zell-Ravenheart's* Grimoire.)

———. *Grimoire for the Apprentice Wizard.* New Page Books, 2004. (*This book, which has been described as a "Boy Scout Handbook for magick users," is rich with "how-tos" and tables of correspondences, planetary hours, rituals, spellwork, and the like.*)

Chapter Five

Filling the Hours

The secret of success in life is to be ready for opportunity when it comes.
—BENJAMIN DISRAELI

You've created a basic format: now it's time to consider what you'll do on your retreat and what you'll need to have on hand. By thinking ahead, you'll be well prepared and your retreat will run smoothly, undisturbed by mundane concerns or worries about details.

Magickal Activities

Magickal activities are those in which we practice craft skills without delving specifically into matters of religion or spirituality—much of magickal practice is craft rather than religion. Now, granted, in many instances the magickal and the spiritual are closely intertwined. But they often appear separately as well. For example, before one can begin studying the runes and incorporating them into spiritual practice, he may wish to make a set for himself. The person who wishes to perfect the ritual raising of energies may first want to craft a wand, but in order to do this he may have to spend time learning to use woodcrafting tools. An alchemist wishing to make spagyric tinctures must first learn to brew infusions and decoctions. And so forth . . .

What sorts of magickal activities will you bring into your retreat? Are you interested in practicing a magickal skill? Improving your powers of observation? Searching and learning the stars? Developing a tool or creating a piece of writing or magickal art? In chapters to come, we'll consider some specific designs for magickal practices. For now, simply think about how you'd like to work with magick during your retreat.

Bringing the elements into your space:

- **Earth:** Earth grounds and provides a center. Use natural stoneware or earthenware on your table. Set stones, rocks, and crystals around your home. Use natural sea salt in your kitchen.

- **Air:** Air is energizing, inspiring, and improves the clarity of the mind. To bring air into your home, open the windows. Burn candles, incense, or essential oils. Hang wind chimes and banners outside your windows. Hang mobiles inside your home.

- **Fire:** Fire is energy in its purest form. To bring in fire, burn candles and smudges. If you have a fireplace, keep a fire burning as a gathering point and a place to meditate. Hang prism-creating crystals in the windows. Cook with fiery spices and peppers.

- **Water:** Water calms, soothes, and heals. One of the best ways to bring water into your space is with a small tabletop fountain; these have the added benefit of releasing negative ions into the surrounding room, creating a sense of peace and well-being. Or, try setting out a bowl of water, with flower petals or floating candles on its surface.

- **Spirit:** Spirit supports energy and emotions, connects us to the world, and inspires us to greater things. For spirit, you may wish to incorporate photographs of your loved ones, or items of family memorabilia. You may wish to display certain books. Emphasize items with great personal meaning.

Spiritual Activities

If magickal activities are all about practicing craft knowledge and skills, you'll use those skills to enrich, expand, or explore your spiritual activities, and you'll probably want to devote at least part of your retreat to spiritual or religious work. You might study coursework toward an initiation, work with prayer or meditation, add content to a spiritual Book of Shadows or Book of Write, or practice ritual or spellwork.

Why am I separating "magickal" and "spiritual"? Granted, they are often so closely related as to be inextricable from one another. I could argue that everything we do is both magickal and spiritual. But I'd like you to try thinking of them as separate-but-equal components, because this will help you tease your ideas apart a little more, which, in turn, will push you to come up with fresh ideas and approaches as you plan your retreat. The easiest way to do this is to imagine the "magickal" as a time of hands-on development and practical skill-building, while the "spiritual" (or religious) is a time of direct, personal application.

Here are some simple ways of adding a spiritual bent to your retreat:

- Bring protective elements or correspondences into the room and charge them with magickal significance: i.e., elemental objects, gems, essential-oil candles, or other items lending protection or magickal contagion.

- Perform a smudging or burn herbs or incense (blessing, purification).

- Scatter salt or dried herbs (purification).

- "Asperge" with salt water or herbal infusions (purification).

- Invoke the power of a patron spirit or of the elements (invocation).

- Clap with your hands throughout the room: this disperses old, stagnant energy (banishment, dispersion).

- Ring a bell or shake a rattle throughout the room: this welcomes in sacred energy (invocation, appeal).

- Cast a circle and work within it (creation of safe and sacred space).

- Bless tools, talismans, or other items (blessing).

- Pray to deity or patron figures (prayer).

- Carry out formal or informal ritual, spellwork, altarcraft, or the like.

Mundane Considerations

Your retreat may be magickal and will almost certainly be spiritual, but it will also encompass the mundane as well. You'll want to consider the mundane elements and make sure they run smoothly, for they'll provide a key support structure to the entire retreat. Simply put, if you're hungry, cold, or uncomfortable, you won't have much fun and it will be challenging to focus on the retreat itself.

Your mundane considerations may include:

- Travel to and from the retreat location
- Physical considerations of the location: Can you drive right up to it, or must you hike or climb to gain access? Is it temperature controlled, or will you be at the mercy of the elements? Is there electricity? Running water? Room service? Indoor plumbing?
- Are there any safety issues that need considering?
- How will you manage food and water?
- What do you need to rest and sleep comfortably?
- Will you need special clothes or gear: for example, walking shoes or a swimsuit?
- What are your emergency and/or safety considerations? Who will know where you are and when you're expected back? How will you get help during the retreat if you need it?

Setting the Mood

As you prepare for your retreat, consider how you'll establish the mood once you're on-site. In thinking "mood," the best approach is often through the senses . . .

Sight

If you have favorite talismans, photographs, crystals, magickal objects, or other personal *tchotchke*, bring them along. Strewn in your work area, they'll provide comfort and inspiration. Ditto for a favorite blanket or altar cloth. A touch of the familiar can be very useful when doing magickal or spiritual work; the recognized object can provide both reference point and anchor—a firm place to return to, as well as a possible focus for grounding and meditation.

Candles add beauty, inspiration, and a touch of the "liminal" to any setting. If using candles during your retreat, keep them on a safe surface and away from anything that could catch fire, and never leave them unattended. A quart-size glass Mason jar makes an excellent candleholder; the clear glass allows full view of the candle, but the candle is completely contained within the jar, and the melted wax cannot spread and start a fire. Screw on the lid and the candle extinguishes itself. Salt (halite) and selenite candleholders are safe (and beautiful) ways to use votives or tealight candles. The new automatic LED candles provide a wonderful touch if your retreat location doesn't allow open flames. You can even use LED candles safely within tents.

Will you be camping outdoors? Nothing sets the mood better than a campfire. Bring dry wood and lots of smaller tinder and kindling to get the fire going. Laundry lint and old bits of candles make superb fire starters. Begin with fire starters and small, dry pieces of wood. As the fire begins burning well, keep adding slightly larger pieces to form a "Teepee" structure; this triangular shape mimics the fire's natural form and burns quickly and easily. When finished with the fire, extinguish until it is "cold out," meaning you can place your hand on the cold ashes and feel no warmth.

Scent

If you like working with scented candles and incense, by all means include them in your retreat. Their scents may provide a textured depth that adds to the setting you've created. And don't forget that fragrances are also powerful in their own right. A scent is the most potent energy trigger known, conjuring up scenes that may be decades old or even connecting us with other times or worlds. Aromas also have the ability to create their own magickal influences; use specially chosen scents to help you meditate, think creatively, invite in your favorite deity, and more.

Touch

Your skin is your largest sensory organ: spend time thinking about how to bring it to life throughout your retreat. Think soft clothes and beddings, fleece jackets, warm hats, fluffy socks for your feet, silk pajamas, soft cotton robes, or whatever feels wonderful to you. Are you planning to soak in a bathtub? Don't forget your favorite silky bath oil. Will you be outdoors? Spend some time going barefoot, allowing your feet to actually touch the earth.

Taste

We'll talk more about food in a bit. But obviously, your retreat is a time to eat and drink in a way that nurtures and enlivens your magickal and spiritual self. As I said, more discussion on this is to come.

Sound

Music can provide a wonderful background or may even become a focus of your retreat. Native American drums and flutes provide a soothing backcloth for meditation and contemplation, as does most Celtic music. Classical music is known to be helpful during periods of intense study, particularly if you listen to Bach, Mozart, or Chopin—apparently their controlled, mathematical nature actually helps one study and retain information. A carefully chosen piece of music can support a magickal mindset and inspire creativity. White noise or sounds taken from nature also work well for some people and are especially good at creating that sense of "other" that's so important in a retreat setting.

Rather than simply using music as a background, you may choose to use it as part of dance or other joyful, ecstatic activity. There's a lot of good "Pagan" and general dance music available these days. As you select, make sure that the energy level matches your intended purpose.

Other ways to use sound: bring a small bell; use it in ritual, or simply ring it as you move from one part of your retreat to the next. The auditory cue provided by the bell adds to the sense of "other" space. Another idea: hang a wind chime where either the wind or your hand can stir it.

Magickal Spidey-Sense ☺

Consider those artifacts and trappings that activate your magickal self and awareness. Perhaps donning robes slips you into magickal space. Maybe you brew a special cup of tea, put on specific music, light candles, or begin with a ritual or incantation. You might even set up a small altar space or a collection of magickal materials. Consider what wakens your magickal senses and provide for these aspects as you plan. After all, your retreat time will be limited, and you'll want to maximize every second of it.

Physical Activity

Physical activity nourishes the body and inspires well-being and creativity. There are a number of ways to work physical activity into your retreat, and I strongly encourage you to do so.

- Begin the day with a brisk walk or run. Leave the iPod behind and listen to and engage with the awakening world around you. Look for a "day sign" (more on this in chapter 6)—a natural augur or occurrence that seems to speak to you. Journal about it when your walk is over, and ponder the augur's meaning.

- If you have private access to workout equipment, or a swimming pool or lake, you could certainly incorporate intentional exercise into your schedule. Avoid the public gym, though, as this would invade and undo the solitude of your retreat. Also, if you normally exercise daily, you may decide *not* to do so during your retreat as a way of emphasizing the difference between your "usual" and "retreat" realms.

- Bring dance into your retreat experience. Dance spontaneously, dance to music, dance in ritual, or spin (carefully) around a campfire. Feel the joy of fluid movement.

- Build one or two walks into your plan. Or, if your routine stagnates or the day seems to slow down, go for an unscheduled walk. Walk quickly enough to perspire or to be on the edge of breathlessness, feeling the blood pumping through you. Slow your pace and breathe deeply of nature's gifts.

- Work with tai chi, yoga, or another healthy art. Don't know tai chi or yoga? Rent or buy an instructional DVD and have fun working this into your retreat. Who knows? A new health routine may be born.

- If you're a bicyclist and there are bike paths or quiet roads nearby, bring your bike along and enjoy an occasional ride. This can be especially fun in an area that is new to you—it's a great way to get the lay of the land. And please wear your helmet! We magick users need to protect our brains.

- Are you planning an outdoor retreat? This would be the perfect time to take a hike. Make sure that someone else knows where you will be hiking and when to expect your return. In addition, carry the Ten Outdoor Essentials. Remember that even a twisted ankle on an outdoor trail could make it impossible for you to walk, leaving you to "survive" until found. The Ten Outdoor Essentials are easy to pack into a corner of your backpack, and they'll keep you warm and safe while you wait. Note: if you hike often, invest in a waist bag or fanny pack to hold the TOEs; that way, whenever you want to head out, just grab it, and you'll be set.

The Ten Outdoor Essentials

1. Weather-appropriate clothing, plus a warm or rainproof jacket and/or a thin metallic "space blanket." (The space blanket can also be used for a rough shelter.)

2. Matches and fire starters—old candle stubs work well. Waterproof the matches by dipping the heads in paraffin and storing the matches in a small tin or an old film canister.

3. Pocketknife

4. Water

5. Food—a granola bar or two

6. Map and compass; a GPS may work, too, but batteries can quit, and there are still places where GPS doesn't work: e.g., deep canyons.

7. First aid kit

8. Flashlight with fresh batteries

9. A plastic whistle (metal ones stick to the lips in freezing conditions)

10. Sunblock or sun protection

Embracing Silence

While music and dance may be an important part of your retreat, many people choose to invoke silence, both internal and external.

Working in a silent setting—no music, no television, no iPod, no smartphone, and no other form of ambient noise—forces one to be more aware of everything and heightens awareness of real and magickal space.

Personal intentional silence—not speaking, singing, or otherwise making sound during the experience—can also be a powerful addition to a time of introspection and meditation. Keeping silence may be used as a type of self-test, particularly if it culminates in initiation or vigil.

Whatever your path or motivations, as a good magick user you should be able to embrace the silence. Listen to it. Welcome it. Hear it. Yes—*hear it*. Silence, after all, makes its own sound. More important, silence—whether external or internal—allows you to hear and respond to your inner voice. It is this voice from which personal growth and insight come. When there's too much noise and activity around us, it can be impossible to hear much of anything, and the still inner voice is lost in the hubbub. An important focus of the retreat experience is in its powers of transformation. While on retreat, you'll listen quietly to your inner wisdom and for those moments of revelation that "gift" you with new understandings.

Silence is an especially valuable tool for those retreating in a natural setting. I'm continually frustrated when I see people walking or working outside while plugged in to MP3 players, making it impossible for them to hear and experience the sounds around them. Staying silent while out in nature will open you to an amazing trove of experiences . . . you'll hear birdsong, the sound of wind in the trees, the movement of squirrels overhead, the crunch of leaves underfoot. Allowing yourself to experience these connections will bring you more deeply into nature's world and open you to possibly transcendent experiences.

The Big Unplug: Separating from the Electronic World

And speaking of silence and listening, here it comes . . .

When I mentioned the words *iPod* and *smartphone* in relationship to silence, you got nervous, didn't you? Well, here it is: unless you're a cybermage and the Internet is an important part of your magickal or spiritual practices (or an intentionally "cyber" retreat), I believe it's important to disconnect yourself completely from the cyberworld during your retreat.

Why? Many reasons.

First, we're living within the time of the digital revolution and digital paradigm shift, and it's causing people to behave strangely.

Go out shopping, and half the people you'll see have cell phones *in their hands.* Not in purses or pockets or backpacks—*in their hands.* Watch them . . . every few seconds, each one is looking down at the screen and often so busy texting or reading that he or she is not bothering to look at what's happening three feet away. I saw an item a few months ago on the evening news about a woman in a mall who was so intent on her cell phone—as she was walking—that she walked right into a sunken pond on the mall's edge! It was hilarious. This water feature was probably twenty feet long, and she didn't even see it coming. I rest my case.

Turn into a "fly on the wall" at the typical restaurant table and too often you'll see each person munching away while staring into the cell phone parked next to the dinner plate—all the while ignoring the real people at the same table.

Slip into a typical home in the evening, and you're likely to find the inhabitants sitting in different rooms in front of screens: cell phones, laptops, video games, and others. And guess what? Once again, they're off in their own worlds, staring into electronic screens while failing to interact with their flesh-and-blood loved ones only a few feet away.

Here's the thing. The digital world is fantastic. I mean, you'll have to pry my laptop out of my cold, dead hands. But when technology pulls us in so deeply that we lose contact with the real three-dimensional world we live in or that we find it hard to function or interact with our fellow humans, then Houston, we have a problem.

Remember that the point of your retreat is for you to focus on yourself in a deeply spiritual and magickal sense. Doing this requires a certain amount of privacy and quiet, both internal and external. It requires uninterrupted time and concentration, and it's almost impossible to find this depth of focus or this kind of private contemplative silence if you remain connected to the digital world—i.e., if you're constantly checking Facebook or sending text messages. Don't get me wrong: I enjoy using the Web as much as anyone. But during your retreat, the focus must be on you and your journey—not on the rest of the universe. Your retreat is designed to be quiet, solitary, and settled. By its very nature, the retreat means you are setting yourself apart. This means you must temporarily detach from the mundane world—and this means in literal *and* digital terms.

Therefore, if we can agree that it's important to disconnect yourself from the cyber-world during your retreat, I propose that these "rules" be part of your retreat:

- No telephone, cell phone, tablet, or anything of the sort. If you feel an absolute need to be in touch with family, let them know that you will check messages (for emergencies only!) once or twice a day, but that you will leave your phone *off* otherwise and will not make or receive phone calls until the retreat ends.

They will need to manage without you while you're gone. (And trust me: they *can* do it.)

- No texting (sending or receiving)
- No e-mail or computer use
- No audiovisual or digital devices, including laptops, tablets, cell phones, television, radio, MP3 players, and similar items
- E-readers, iPods, tablets, or laptops may be okay *if* they hold texts or music that you will use during your retreat, but you *must* avoid the temptation to surf and send e-mail! I would suggest you avoid using any of these devices unless you really have no other option.

You get the idea: the goal is to disconnect yourself from the electronic world as part of your retreat. Believe me: everyone will be okay without hearing from you for a day or two, and you'll be fine, too. In pre-cell phone and pre-answering machine days, humans relied on plain old phones and still managed to get in touch with each other when they really needed to. Disconnecting briefly from modern culture and everyday communication removes you from the mundane routines of your usual life and helps you enter the world of "other," the liminal space that defines your hero's journey and your spiritual retreat.

Parting company with electronics is also an excellent way to engage with silence. In today's digital age, we are continually barraged with visual and auditory images, and as a result, most people today don't understand silence. Their ears are continually occupied with personal music systems, cell phones, and the like, and their eyes with video screens, television, etc. One can neither listen well nor hear well in the midst of this kind of noise and sensory overload. Imagine, for instance, trying to meditate effectively while texting or playing a video game!

There's also mounting neuropsychological evidence that the "bites" (and bytes) of information we process through electronic means are affecting the way we think and may even be interfering with our ability to read dense, complex texts. We're seeing this particularly in young people, who are used to receiving a constant stream of digital information but who have increasing difficulty reading a long sustained piece of work, such as a novel. Brain imaging shows that different parts of the brain are activated by different activities; reading a short blurb on the Web makes one portion light up, while reading *The Lord of the Rings* or *War and Peace* activates a different region entirely. For those of us interested in magick and earth-based spirituality, much of our development comes through reading and study. The moral of the story: use it or lose it! Enjoy your Internet, but keep reading those long, dense, challenging books as well.

About Multitasking

Let's talk about another benefit of your retreat: namely, it will allow you to slow down and focus intently on one thing at a time. Why is this important?

We live in a fast-paced, digital environment, and most of us spend a significant part of our day juggling digital devices and soaking up electronic input. The key word there is *juggling*. It's not unusual for us to try and do several tasks at once. Perhaps you cook dinner with an eye on the television news while simultaneously checking voicemail on your cell phone, reading text messages, and helping your child with homework. Or, you might sit down at your laptop to check e-mails or work on a piece of writing only to find yourself scanning Facebook or surfing the Web. Most of us think we're pretty good at this. We believe ourselves to be successful "multitaskers," and we see this as a way to get several things done at once.

The problem is, we're wrong.

In his article "Myth of Multitasking," University of San Francisco professor Jim Taylor remarks, "The fact is that multitasking, as most people understand it, is a myth that has been promulgated by the 'technological-industrial complex' to make overly scheduled and stressed-out people feel productive and efficient." Taylor goes on to explain that we're actually carrying out serial tasking rather than multitasking, and that in doing so, we not only lose efficiency but wear ourselves out. Taylor's claims are backed by Stanford University researcher Eyal Ophir (et. al.), and these two pieces of research are only the tip of an emerging iceberg that's just poking its nose above the technological waterline.

Yes, the research is in, and it proves that we really *can't* multitask. We think we're multitasking, but in reality, we're simply switching from one task to another so rapidly that we don't realize we're doing it. So, you're thinking . . . what's the problem? The problem is that the act of rapidly switching every few minutes (or seconds) between one task and the next actually *slows us down*. Brain scanning shows that this switching actually "splits" the brain, assigning tasks to different areas; this makes the activity much less efficient than it normally would be and also has a profound dis-organizing effect on the brain. It ends up taking us longer, collectively, to complete each task than it would if we tackled them one at a time. The same research shows that we cannot effectively handle more than two tasks "at once," and even then, we aren't handling them simultaneously. Not surprisingly, multitasking causes us to do a worse job at each activity and leaves us much less likely to retain a sound memory of the activity or its results. It's also exhausting.

Yikes.

So why this myth of multitasking? Why do we believe we're so good at it, and why has modern culture seemingly begun to focus on multitasking as an expected part of life? The simplest answer probably looks squarely at the digital revolution. Our days have become fast-paced and packed with a steady information flow; we try to keep up by doing several things at once, with the results being mediocre comple-tion, fragmented memory, heightened stress, and escalating fatigue. And of course, this only brings us back to the need for spiritual silence and sanctuary.

Your retreat provides you with an opportunity to slow down and experience the joyful calm of tackling one thing at a time. Embrace this as an intentional part of your retreat. Develop a schedule that allows you the luxury of focusing on one activ-ity at a time, enjoying the ease of simple, unencumbered time. If you plan to make the digital world part of your retreat, try focusing on one aspect at a time. Whatever you do on your retreat, slow down and give it your full, undivided attention.

Introverts and Extroverts

Do you consider yourself an introvert or an extrovert? Either way, it's worth consid-ering when planning a retreat. Let's note that being an introvert doesn't mean that one doesn't like being around people. Not at all. What it means is that the introvert must spend time by herself in order to recharge and re-gather her own energy level. An extrovert, on the other hand, recharges best when surrounded by others and may feel weak and a bit empty or lost if he spends a long stretch of time on his own.

These characteristics cause different people to approach a retreat experience in different ways, and this presents unique challenges on each side. For introverts, being alone is already comfortable and energizing; these folks may find the idea of a re-treat obvious and may need to dig deep to make the undertaking surpass the kinds of experiences they already have every day. In other words, if you already recharge within your own silence, how do you "extend" or deepen that to make a retreat that feels somehow different from everyday life? Crafting a vigil or vision quest experience might be a good example of how to extend one's usual introverted-ness into a profound experience.

In contrast, extroverts often prefer to be around people 24/7 and may view being alone as boring or even a bit terrifying. They may need reassurance that a *personal* retreat can be fun and worthwhile. The extrovert may benefit from beginning with a shorter retreat, allowing him to test the waters, so to speak. The extrovert may also be most comfortable if he includes lots of visual and auditory input in his experience or if he retreats in an area where people are nearby, within seeing distance. He might also plan occasional forays into the community, perhaps visiting a library or coffee shop to soak in human vibes.

The tasks for this chapter will suggest that you take a Myers-Briggs personality inventory. The Myers-Briggs test uses a series of questions about how one responds in a specific setting or situation. When the answers are combined, the test presents a sort of profile, showing how the subject perceives the world, interacts with others, and makes decisions. Taking this test is a fascinating way to learn more about yourself as well as how you interact with others.

Meditation

When one is in the midst of a personal vision experience, many insights will come through intentional inward focus or meditation. It's that idea of silence again—of being silent so you can both listen and *hear*. I recommend that a good portion of your retreat should be spent in quiet, contemplative thought and meditation (see chapter 3). How you incorporate this is up to you, but I suggest meditating each morning upon arising, each night before bed, and before and after key activities.

- In the morning, focus on the day to come. Clear your mind and see what messages or inspirations come.

- Meditating before and after magickal or spiritual activities may provide insights, revelations, or new perspectives. Journal about your discoveries, and consider how these ideas teach or strengthen you.

• Performing a simple meditation before sleep helps clear your mind of the day's thoughts and prepares a "blank slate" for your dream life. Think of it as a pre-sleep reboot.

People who are experienced with meditation may choose to spend large segments of the retreat meditating, using it as a key focus of the experience.

Feast or Fast?

Food can fill any role in your retreat experience. Depending on your focus, you may choose to feast, fast, or anything in between. Feasting can be a joyful part of your retreat, while fasting can add to the spiritual nature and may leave your mind feeling sharper and more clear than usual. You might even merge the two, beginning the retreat with simple fasting and finishing with a celebratory banquet. The choice, of course, is yours.

If you choose to eat regular meals, give some thought to the types of foods you'll choose. I recommend that you stick to unprocessed, natural, or organic foods; doing this and keeping the meals simple and rather ascetic may add to the feeling of "specialness" during the experience. On the other hand, if you love to cook, you can work that into your plan and go all out. In fact, foodies may want to cook up a storm during a retreat, enjoying the luxury of available time. Some of you might eschew my suggestion to go organic and unprocessed. A technomage friend of mine feasted on caffeinated soda, pepperoni pizza, pretzels, and cheap canned beer throughout her retreat.

Some people turn to fasting to lend a special effect to their retreats. There's support behind this: many esoteric traditions include fasting as an accepted practice, believing that fasting sharpens the senses and creates a "hungry mind." The practice makes sense from a physiological perspective, too. Fatty foods fill one's bloodstream with fatty lipids shortly after the food is consumed. Imagine that you consumed a high-fat meal that included a rich, fat-dense piece of meat, buttered vegetables, and a potato with butter and sour cream. If a tube of blood was drawn from your arm shortly after, and if that tube was allowed to rest, the blood cells would settle to the bottom of the tube, and the blood serum—the liquid part of the blood—would actually look cloudy and white. We call this "lipemic serum" (literally "fat blood") because the white cloudiness comes from the fat globules temporarily filling the bloodstream after a fat-dense meal. As you might expect, this creates a sludgy condition within the blood vessels and within your organs—including your brain. Circulation is impaired and mental functions suffer—this is why we always feel sleepy after eating a rich, heavy meal. Eating low-fat foods or simply eating lightly keeps the circulating fat levels low and improves one's alertness, concentration, and focus.

If you decide to fast, proceed with care. If you have past experience with fasts, rely on that—but keep in mind that you'll be busy and probably trying to accomplish a number of tasks during your retreat. If fasting, I would suggest that you work with a juice fast rather than water only. Juices provide carbohydrates, which should help you stay energized and avoid plunging your body into a ketotic state where it begins burning muscle tissue. If you start to feel weak or terribly hungry, please eat! Sustaining the fast isn't worth undermining your retreat experience, and, after all, your food intake (or lack thereof) isn't the reason why you're retreating. If you want to incorporate fasting at some point, one option might be to fast briefly in conjunction with a special part of the retreat: for example, prior to and during a vigil fire. If fasting is new to you, consult expert resources before trying it—and you should probably try it at least once *before* your retreat to see how you respond.

However you plan them, your food plans—like everything else that happens during your retreat— should spring from intention, including what you eat and drink. Here are a few general suggestions to help you eat and drink "mindfully":

1. Eat lightly and simply and eat only enough to feel satisfied. Offer a prayer or blessing before you eat. Chew slowly and meditate on the way that the food is restoring your body as you eat. These simple actions alone can improve the type of food you eat and the way you eat it.

2. Emphasize natural foods that are lightly prepared, if prepared at all. Steamed or raw vegetables, raw fruits, juices, cooked oatmeal, skim dairy products, artisan bread, organic nut butters, and plain chicken or fish are perfect examples. Focus on highly colored foods (broccoli, sweet potatoes, purple grapes, etc.) as these are full of antioxidants. Avoid saturated fats and trans fats (read the labels: if it says "partially hydrogenated" anywhere, you have a trans fat), processed or premade foods, refined sugar, high-fructose corn syrup (which is *not* the same

as sugar), and artificial sweeteners. As food journalist Michael Pollan suggests, "Avoid anything your grandmother wouldn't recognize as food."

3. Go lightly with caffeine and alcohol. Neither is terribly harmful on its own—in fact, some health research shows benefits from both caffeine and alcohol when used in moderation. But understand that caffeine is a powerful stimulant as well as a water-depleting diuretic. As for alcohol, it's a potent central nervous system depressant, a mild diuretic, and—technically—a chemical poison that has been shown to damage or even kill nerve and brain cells when used in larger-than-moderate quantities. Enjoy these beverages, but don't overdo them.

4. Don't eat just because it's "time"; eat when you're hungry, and eat slowly and lightly—taking in just enough to feel full. For some of you, this may mean you only eat twice a day; others might eat every two hours. If hunger is an issue, try several light snacks throughout the day. In any case, the goal is not to eat because the clock says, "It's time," but to eat when your body speaks to you, telling you it needs nourishment. Eating slowly is important, too. From the time we swallow our first bite of food, it takes the stomach/brain connection up to twenty minutes to register the food intake. Therefore, eating slowly will help you be satisfied with less.

5. On the other hand, some people include food and meals as a "treat" aspect of the retreat, eating whenever and whatever they choose. This is fine, too. Remember: it's all about the retreat you're designing and about you making it deeply personal.

6. When you cook or eat, make it into a ritual. Do as much of the food preparation by hand as you can—tear the lettuce leaves, slice the fruits and veggies, even bake the bread if you feel like it. Sit down to a table set with tableware and at least one candle. Play soft music. Make the meal into a ritual by washing your hands before coming to the table and offering thanks for the food before you eat. Wash your hands again when you finish and recite a blessing; this closes the meal and helps remind you of the sacredness of the act.

7. Don't read or engage in any other activity while eating: be mindful of the act of eating in and of itself, and visualize the food and drink restoring your body.

8. Drink water throughout the retreat, aiming for at least a cup of water every couple of hours. Chances are you may not drink this much water in your everyday life, and you'll be surprised at how it rejuvenates you. Non-caffeinated herbal teas and natural fruit juices can be substituted for water.

Don't forget the magick inherent in the foods. Like everything else in the world, foods come with their own magickal energies, natures, and actions. Working with the attributes of specific foods, herbs, and beverages will allow you to use these qualities to support your own intentions.

Packing Up

If you'll be working in your home, you'll have your materials at hand. However, you should still gather them into a single place, so that you won't have to spend valuable retreat time searching for your wand or clean robes or scrying crystals or whatever else you need.

For an away-from-home retreat, you'll need to pack as you would for any trip. Consider the following general lists:

Personal items

- Clothes (including day wear, exercise clothes, and weather-appropriate outerwear)
- Footwear (shoes, boots, slippers)
- Toiletry items (towel and washcloth, soap, shampoo, deodorant, toothbrush and toothpaste)
- Medications (bring along some aspirin or ibuprofen, too—just in case)
- Eyeglasses or contact lenses (including spares, cleaning materials, etc.)
- Exercise materials
- Purse/wallet and identification, such as a driver's license

Safety items

- Flashlight and extra batteries
- First aid kit
- Cell phone and charger (turned *off*)

Food and drink

- Food
- Pots, pans, and cooking utensils
- Plates, cups, and personal utensils
- Kitchen towels and napkins

Magickal items

- Ritual jewelry and garb
- A portable altar setup: see the description of "Altoid altars" in chapter 10
- Books and reference materials
- Journal
- Specific items for your magickal retreat activities

Mundane items

- Camera
- Desk supplies (pens, pencils, sticky notes, etc.)
- Books
- Music
- Electronics and charger (only if essential for music or other materials)
- Specific items for your mundane retreat activities

Miscellany

- Camping gear
- Portable camping chair
- Small cooler for food
- Money
- Matches
- Candles
- Firewood

Make good lists, and check them at least twice . . .

Filing a Trip Plan

If you're leaving your home to go on retreat, it's imperative that you let at least one other person know where you're going, how you're getting there, the dates you'll be gone, when to expect you back, and how to contact you in case of emergency. This is especially important if you live alone. Write this information down and make two copies. Keep the original "trip plan" with you throughout the retreat; give a copy to a friend, neighbor, or family member; and stick the other copy up on your refrigerator.

You'll find a trip plan template in Appendix B.

Ensuring Seclusion

In order that you can do the work you need to do, you cannot be distracted, and that's why you are on retreat *alone*. If you're leaving family and friends behind for a day or two (or more), never fear: they will be absolutely fine, and you'll return with a rested, happy soul, ready to plunge back into those relationships.

Let your loved ones know that you won't be available during the retreat. Arrange a plan to check for phone messages once or twice a day, but let them know you will not reply unless the situation is truly an emergency. And yes, checking only once or twice a day is more than sufficient. Keep in mind that we had telephones for decades without even having answering machines, and everyone still managed to stay in touch. Relax and enjoy your time away, and be sure to bring your loved ones a treat on the way home.

Tasks for Chapter 5

The journey continues . . . and the excitement builds. No doubt your retreat will come with its own challenges, which you'll hopefully meet with joy. Planning ahead will help the road be smooth, and a bit of divine inspiration can't hurt, either.

1. At the center of this retreat is work with magick and/or spirituality. What sorts of activities have you decided to focus on? How will these strengthen you? What will you gain or learn?

_____

_____

_____

_____

2. Will you follow your own lead or seek guidance from deity, spirits, or patrons while on retreat? How will this enrich or direct your experience?

_____

_____

_____

_____

3. How will you create a mood and setting for your retreat?

_____

_____

_____

_____

4. How will you embrace silence?

_____

_____

_____

_____

5. How do you respond to the idea of going electronically silent? Write about your response to the suggestion.

_____

_____

_____

_____

6. Make a list of food and drink that you will have on hand during your retreat. Write one or two paragraphs that describe the kind of meals that you plan for the experience.

_____

_____

_____

_____

7. Use a search engine to search for "Myers-Briggs." The Myers-Briggs test is a personality inventory that will tell you a lot about how you interact with others, as well as whether you are more introverted or extroverted. Take the test and consider your results. What did you discover? Were you surprised at all?

_____

_____

_____

_____

8. Will you feast, fast, or something in between? Explain how you'll work with food and drink during your retreat.

_____

_____

_____

_____

Notes and Ideas:

_____

_____

_____

_____

Suggested Resources for This Chapter

Alexander, Jane. *Sacred Rituals at Home.* Sterling, 2000.

Drew, A. J. *A Wiccan Formulary and Herbal.* New Page Books, 2004.

Ophir, Eyal, Clifford Nass, and Anthony D. Wagner. "Cognitive Control in Media Multitaskers." *Proceedings of the National Academy of Sciences*, July 2009. Online at http://www.pnas.org/content/early/2009/08/21/0903620106.full.pdf+html.

Pollan, Michael. *Food Rules: An Eater's Manual.* Penguin, 2009.

Taylor, Jim. "Myth of Multitasking." *Huffington Post*, March 31, 2011. Online at http://www.huffingtonpost.com/dr-jim-taylor/myth-of-multitasking_b_842550.html.

Telesco, Patricia. *A Kitchen Witch's Cookbook.* Llewellyn, 2002.

Chapter Six

Solitude and Mindfulness

In solitude, where we are least alone.
—LORD BYRON

To be mindful of something is to be consciously aware of it—in other words, not to just passively receive or experience a presence or action, but to actively participate in or be part of it.

We toss the term around loosely. For example, we might ask our child or spouse to be "mindful" of the electricity wasted when the lights are left on. But when talking about magick and spiritual practices, we mean something on a deeper level. The gist of the conversation changes from one of passive reception to active involvement.

The English word *mindfulness* has been in use since at least the thirteenth century. The *Oxford English Dictionary* not only defines words but also tracks their usage over time. The *OED* defines *mindfulness* as "the state or quality of being mindful; attention; regard," and also includes related definitions of the words *intention, memory,* and *purpose*. According to the *OED*, the word was first recorded as the obsolete "mindiness" (ca. 1200), as "mindful" in 1340, "mindfully" in 1382, "myndfulness" in 1530, "mindfulnesse" in 1561, and "mindfulness" in 1817.

The idea of mindfulness takes on great importance in Buddhist practices, where it is the seventh element of the Eightfold Path leading to spiritual enlightenment. The Buddhists describe mindfulness as a calm, watchful, focused awareness of internal and external conditions, consciousness, and perceptions. It is absolutely an active process rather than a passive one. The passive *recipient* simply allows life to happen to him; the mindful *participant* engages actively with the process, and through this, hopes not only to benefit but also to reach that point of universal enlightenment and understanding.

Teachings written in Sanskrit refer to mindfulness as "that which is remembered," and view the practice as an important part of recalling and connecting with ancestral teachings and authorities. Chinese and Tibetan practices incorporate some sort of mindful awareness, vigilance, or attention into their teachings as well. I've always viewed mindfulness as expressed well in the saying "Be here, now," which is attributed to the Western-born yogi and spiritual teacher Ram Dass. It's such a simple statement but so very true.

Practicing Mindfulness

Becoming more mindful is a boon to any type of magickal and spiritual practice and will enrich your retreat experience as well. The easiest way to begin working with this is simply to practice consciously throughout one's day. For example:

- When first waking in the morning: Before looking at the clock, thinking about the day's "To Do" list, or engaging with the mundane world, take a deep breath and simply "be present in" your body. Be aware of anything that feels particularly warm or cold, including the toasty area under the covers. Feel the weight of gravity pressing your body down onto the mattress, and feel the gentle weight of the bedding over you. Move your limbs slowly, contracting each muscle group from toes to forehead and experiencing the fluidity (or morning stiffness) of that movement. Rejoice in the gift of being able to move those muscles. Take a deep breath and feel the life force moving within you.

- When eating, turn off or disable television, music, cell phone, and other distractions. Set an attractive table and "be present" at the table with your food.

Take a single bite and chew slowly; feel the food being chewed away to a pulp inside your mouth. Experience the textures and flavors. As you swallow, visualize the vitamins and nutrients in the food nourishing and strengthening your body.

- When outdoors: Stand, sit, or walk quietly by yourself. If possible, be barefoot—too many of us go for months and even years without actually standing on *earth*. Feel the sun's warmth, the rain's wetness, the kiss of breeze. Consider how your feet feel as you walk through grass or along pavement. Concentrate on the pull of breath as you exert, and feel your heart beating and the perspiration springing to your skin as you pick up the pace. Focus on your surroundings, appreciating the colors of leaves and flowers, the clouds, the song of birds. Look at the environment with fresh eyes; make it a habit—every time you walk outdoors—to see something you have not seen or noticed before.

- Anytime/anywhere: Pause and take three deep, slow breaths. Feel your body and be aware of your mind. Step into liminal space for those moments and experience being a conscious, aware being alive in the cosmos.

Many people use visual or auditory cues as reminders to practice mindfulness throughout the day. For example, you might be "triggered" to pause for a mindful moment at any of these times:

- When you step over a threshold
- When you sit down to eat
- When you reach a street corner
- When you climb into your car
- When you see anything red
- When you hear a clock or church bells chime
- When you spot the evening star

One writer friend sets an hourly timer on her iPod Touch. Every hour, when the timer sounds (she uses a harp sound for the "alarm"), she pauses for a moment of mindful awareness or meditation.

Using Prayers and Other Intercessions

Prayers, blessings, and dedications also may help one enter a place of mindfulness. The cadence, intention, and tone of these pieces of spoken magick come with a built-in seriousness that pulls us out of real-time and instantly transports us into "other." Find prayers and other devotions that work for you and incorporate them into your retreat. You might also choose to spend your retreat writing some of your own: see my book *Crafting Magick with Pen and Ink* (listed in the Resources section at the end of this chapter) for guidance with this.

The Day Sign

One lovely way of practicing intentional mindfulness is to look for a "day sign"—a natural augur or occurrence that speaks to you in some way. Go for a walk or simply step outside, preferably first thing in the morning. As you walk or wait, open your powers of observation and wait for the universe to speak to you in some way. There's no predicting how this message will arrive. You might hear birdsong or see a flyover; you might spot an attractive stone, an unusual plant, or see a spider web reaching across tree branches; you might see a rainbow or a unique cloud formation. When something captures your attention, you will have found your day sign. Stop for a moment, feel it, and consider the message it is sending to you. Once you return from your walk, journal about the experience. Come back to the journal one day, one week, and one month later to reread and reflect on its meaning. Over time, you'll come to understand how day signs speak to you.

The day sign can also be used as a kind of active augury—i.e., a way to receive answers or support through a natural sign. Rather than simply opening your mind, begin your walk with a specific question in mind. Think about what issue you would like to resolve or what it is that calls for guidance. Take your walk and watch for the day sign; once found, consider how it responds to your question or concern.

Watching for day signs is one way of practicing and heightening your skills of observation, which is important for all kinds of magick users. See chapter 8 for more about using and developing your powers of observation.

Embracing Slowness

Set a careful, mindful pace and refuse to rush. Work with a plan in mind, making your movements precise and measured. Do one thing at a time, and leave multitasking at the door. You'll be surprised at how much more present you'll feel simply by slowing down. It's a lot like trying to be stressed in a hot bath—i.e., it's almost impossible. The same thing can happen when you make yourself slow down and simplify: the act itself can reinforce the mindset, and the mindset inspires the act.

Embracing Simplicity

Take what you need on retreat, but don't overpack. Be easy with yourself. Have you ever noticed how differently you feel when surrounded by mess and clutter as compared to working in an organized, tidy space? An uncluttered surrounding supports a focused, clear mind. Be prepared, but don't overdo it.

Embracing Timelessness

Follow your schedule, but try not to be ruled by the clock. Stop from time to time and see if you can tell—by your intuition and feelings, the level of daylight, the sense of passing time—what time it is without looking at the clock. Becoming more aware of how time passes is an important part of mindfulness. Magick works better when we control the time rather than it controlling us. If you wear a wristwatch, tuck it away where it's rather hard to get to.

Embracing Mundane Reality

Listen to and respect your body's rhythms while on retreat. Eat well, get some exercise every day, and sleep and nap as needed. Luxuriate in the chance to pay undivided attention to yourself. Focusing on the needs of your mind and body is part of directed intention, because in today's rapid-paced world, we often find ourselves scrambling to care for everyone *but* ourselves.

Embracing Magick

Magick is all about intention, too. To do good magick requires strong powers of observation, focus, and concentration. Take care of the details before you begin a magickal work; this will allow you to focus on the magick itself, rather than the trappings. As you begin the work, open your senses and your powers of observation and see yourself as part of everything that surrounds you. Concentrate on your process—be part of it, immersed in it, swimming in it, rather than standing outside watching it.

Embracing Fun

Don't forget to simply have fun on retreat, too. Consider this a reward for the work you're putting into the journey and especially the intentional aspects. What does "fun" mean? Bring a book to read just for pleasure. Work a jigsaw puzzle. Make chalk drawings on the sidewalk, or blow soap bubbles.

In Summary: Being Mindful

As you prepare to embark upon your retreat, keep mindfulness at the forefront of your considerations. Come to your retreat with a "beginner's mind," free of preconceived ideas and with heart, mind, and spirit open and receptive. Be prepared not only to undertake the goals you have set for yourself but also to learn and possibly to receive gifts from the universe—which has much to teach you. Keep in mind that there is no use undertaking any challenge—including this retreat—if you feel you already know everything and there's nothing more to learn.

Tasks for Chapter 6

I hope this chapter has given you some food for thought, because the idea of working mindfully is probably one of the very most important factors in your retreat's success. Consider the following questions:

1. Assess your own skills at working with intention. Is this something you're good at, or is it something you need to learn more about? Explain your thoughts.

_____

_____

_____

_____

2. How will you consider slowness, simplicity, and timelessness in your retreat?

_____

_____

_____

_____

3. Will these ideas prove easy or difficult? Why?

_____

_____

_____

_____

4. What does mindfulness mean to you?

_____

_____

_____

_____

5. How will you mark that moment when you step over the "threshold" and begin your retreat journey?

_____

_____

_____

_____

Notes and Ideas

_____

_____

_____

_____

Suggested Resources for This Chapter

Daimler, Morgan. *By Land, Sea, and Sky: A Selection of Repaganized Prayers and Charms from Volumes 1 & 2 of the Carmina Gadelica.* Lulu, 2010.

Dalai Lama (His Holiness the). *365: Daily Advice from the Heart.* ThorsonElement, 2001. (*A wonderful little book of daily meditations.*)

Gelb, Michael J. *How to Think Like Leonardo da Vinci*. Delta, 2004. (*A wonderful book that explains da Vinci's seven-step explanation of intentional learning, creativity, and personal growth.*)

Mosley, Ivo, ed. *Earth Poems: Poems from Around the World to Honor the Earth*. HarperSanFrancisco, 1996.

Pesznecker, Susan. *Crafting Magick with Pen and Ink: Learn to Write Stories, Spells, and Other Magickal Works*. Llewellyn, 2009.

Roberts, Elizabeth and Elias Amidon, eds. *Life Prayers: 365 Prayers, Blessings, and Affirmations to Celebrate the Human Journey*. HarperSanFrancisco, 1996.

Serith, Ceisiwr. *A Book of Pagan Prayer*. Weiser, 2002. (*A lovely collection of Pagan-oriented prayers and blessings for all occasions from the casual to the celebratory.*)

Part III

Departure,
Initiation,
and Return

*What lies behind us and what lies before us
are tiny matters compared to what lies within us.*
—RALPH WALDO EMERSON

Chapter Seven

Building a Retreat

The universe is full of magical things, patiently waiting for our wits to grow sharper.
—EDEN PHILLPOTTS

It's getting close! If you've been working through the questions, a framework of ideas is now in place for your retreat, and you're ready to fill in the details.

Since magick-users of all stripes work with herbs, I've used "herbal workings" in creating these samples. If you know how to brew an infusion, you can use it for all sorts of magickal applications. For example, you could drink it to alter your mental state, use it to anoint and consecrate tools, carry out a bit of alchemical spagyrics, sprinkle (asperge) a space for purification, or use the infusion for a healing purpose. Working with herbs is a magickal skill that can be applied to a wide range of spiritual practices.

About the Retreat Template

Each sample retreat plan is set up using a retreat template. The left column highlights specific planning points—everything from Campbell's journey stages to mundane items, like what food and materials to include. These points will help you consider each part of the retreat; you, of course, can decide which ones to use, and depending on your own goals, you might use all of them or might choose only a few. The right column provides space for you to capture your own notes and ideas, make lists, and so forth. A blank template is available in Appendix B at the back of the book, ready to be photocopied for your own use.

Plan for a Mini-Retreat

This bare-bones retreat is only an hour long and includes the brewing of a nice cup of magickal tea and the reading of tea leaves. Short but sweet, this could be just the thing to allow one to unwind and enjoy some private time, and it also should whet the appetite for a longer getaway.

Call to adventure:	I'd like to learn more about working with herbs.
Type of focus:	Testing and trial.
Magickal goals for this retreat:	I'd like to make and use a fresh peppermint infusion.
Time:	Right after work, before anyone gets home.
Place:	My kitchen.
Timing details:	Monday—it's a good time for new beginnings, and that's what this is for me.
Magickal activities:	Making infusions is a skill I can use in all kinds of magick. I might be able to read the tea leaves, too.
Spiritual activities:	None
Mundane activities:	A peppermint infusion also makes an enjoyable tea! I can enjoy this anytime.
Creating mood:	I'll burn a ginger-scented candle to add atmosphere and encourage success.
Embracing silence, slowness, and a quiet pace:	I'll work quietly and think about what I am doing.
Food:	None needed—but I'll be drinking my tea!

Materials needed:	Ginger-scented candle, saucer, matches, fresh peppermint (green grocer), sharp knife, cutting board, small saucepan, tea cup with saucer, spoon, one or two herbal books, paper, pen or pencil, candle extinguisher.
Departure (more on this in chapter 8):	Washing up, changing clothes, lighting a candle.
Schedule:	3:30: Arrive home–put work things in a separate room. Wash hands and face. Change shirt. 3:45: Think about each step and what I'm going to do, mentally casting myself into sacred space. Light candle as I gather intention. 3:50: Boil water. Chop peppermint coarsely and put in cup. When water boils, pour over herbs. Cover with saucer. Set timer to steep 5 minutes. While the mixture brews, practice mindfulness and/or meditation. 3:56: Settle into my favorite chair by the front window, bringing candle along, too. Study the entries on "peppermint" in one or two of my herbal books, taking notes as I read. 4:25: I'll finish last sips of tea, leaving just enough to swirl the tea leaves. Study and "read" the marc (the "spent" tea leaves). Make notes on any results or discoveries. 4:30: I'll take a deep breath, literally "inspiring" the experience. I'll speak a few words of closure–I think "Go in peace" would serve well. Then I'll extinguish the candle and tidy everything up.
Return (more on this in chapter 9):	I'll finish the tea, then will offer thanks for the lesson as I extinguish the candle. I'll clean up everything, and the mini-retreat will be finished.

Plan for a Daylong Retreat

This retreat will fill the space of a "work day," allowing time to work with a number of fresh and dried herbs, engage in study, go for a walk, have a simple meal, and begin work on a herbal formulary—a reference of one's herbal workings. The retreat includes magickal components and ends with a simple ritual.

Here's how that daylong plan might look for those who like super-detailed outlines and planning:

Call to adventure:	I'd like to learn more about working with herbs.
Type of focus:	Practice, testing, and trial.
Magickal goals:	I'd like to make and use at least three different infusions, working with fresh and dried herbs. I'd like to practice using my new mortar and pestle. I'd also like to do some reading and start an herbal formulary notebook. I might make some flash cards, too, for studying my herbs.
Time:	I will start at 8:30 a.m., after everyone has left for the day. I'll finish by 4:30, before anyone gets home.
Place:	The kitchen and dining room table.
Timing details:	Monday—it's a good time for new beginnings, and that's what this is for me.
Magickal activities:	Making infusions is a skill I can use in all kinds of magick. I'll use drinkable herbs and will enjoy the infusions I make as "tea." I'd also like to use at least one to anoint some magickal tools. I'd like to read the tea leaves, too.
Spiritual activities:	A cleansing shower, clean clothes, and a blessing activity to start the day; a blessing over the food at lunch; a ritual closing to the retreat.
Mundane activities:	I'll take an after-lunch walk and see how many herbs I can spot growing in the neighborhood.
Creating mood:	While working with the herbs, I'll burn a ginger-scented candle to add atmosphere and encourage success. I'll play some of my favorite Celtic CDs.
Embracing silence, slowness, and a quiet pace:	I'll work silently and think about what I am doing. Cell phone will be off and in another room. Television will be off. Laptop will be available if I need to find any herbal information, but I'll have my herbal guides available and will use them first.
Food:	Lunch: Artisan bread, cheeses, hummus, apple, and grapes. Afternoon snack: Some lemon cookies to go with my tea.

Materials needed:	*Frankincense soap; ginger-scented candle, saucer, matches, and candle extinguisher; fresh peppermint, rosemary, and sage (green grocer); dried peppermint, rosemary, and sage (prepared a few days in advance from fresh); sharp knife, cutting board; small saucepan and measuring spoons; food scale; infuser basket; mortar and pestle; tea cups with saucers; herbal guidebooks, paper, pen, and colored pencils; blank journal (for formulary); magickal journal; Celtic CDs; lunch materials, plus plate and knife; magickal tools (wand?); printed handout on tasseomancy; ritual*
Departure (more on this in chapter 8):	*As soon as everyone leaves the house, I'll turn off my phone and will shower, using frankincense soap for purification and doing a three-dip ritual.*
	8:45: Think about each step and what I'm going to do, mentally casting myself into sacred space. I'll ground and center, then will light a candle as I gather intention. I'll meditate on my goals and purposes for several minutes, then will center again and will be ready to start. *9:00: I'll pour water over my hands in a ritual of cleansing. I'll start the music and will set out the materials for making the infusions.* *9:10: I'll prepare the first two infusions, using the same herb in fresh and dried forms. Fresh herbs will be coarsely chopped, while dry herbs will be reduced in the mortar and pestle. I'll boil water and pour over herbs, then will cover with a saucer and steep 5 minutes. While the mixture brews, I'll practice mindfulness and silence.* *9:20: Settling into my favorite chair by the front window, I'll sip and compare the first two infusions. As I do, I'll read the sections in the guidebooks about each herb, and I'll capture notes comparing the fresh and dried versions and journal about any modifications to the recipe.*

Schedule: continued	9:45: I'll finish by reading the tea leaves. I'll journal about any discoveries and might make sketches as well.
	9:50: I'll prepare the second set of infusions, following the same process as above.
	10:30: Third set of infusions.
	11:10: I'll settle down at the dining room table and journal about my overall results. I'll ask myself what I have learned through the morning's experiments and will make notes about what new questions have been raised. I'll consider the tasseomancy results, too. Finally, I'll begin outlining a format for my formulary, deciding how to set up each page and what information to include.
	11:45: Lunch.
	12:15: Walk outside for 30 minutes-rain or shine-while watching for herbs growing "wild" or cultivated.
	12:45: Back to work; this time creating the infusions again and experimenting with mixing and matching them into different combinations, whether for taste or magickal utility.
	1:30: Clean up kitchen, reserving a small amount of rosemary infusion and a drinkable portion of my favorite combination.
	1:45: Spread out on dining room table and spend a good two hours developing my herbal formulary, or at least the start of it. It will include magickal and mundane information about each herb, recipes and processes, etc. As I work, I'll create flash cards, too.
	3:45: Tea break with reserved infusion and lemon cookies.
	4:00: Tidy up the space. Repeat a ritual hand-washing and re-enter sacred space.

| Schedule continued | 4:05: Set up a simple elemental altar space on the dining room table: mortar and pestle for "earth," dried herbs for air, the candle for "fire," and the reserved rosemary infusion for "water." In the center of the altar space, I'll place my new formulary. I'll call the quarters and will then dip my fingers into the infusion, sprinkling a few drops over my formulary journal as I ask silently for divine inspiration and guidance. I'll meditate on this for a moment, then will speak a few words of closure (these will be the first words I've spoken all day, and will signal my re-entry into the "usual" world. Finally, I'll end the ritual by extinguishing the candle. |
| Return (more on this in chapter 9): | After extinguishing the candle, I'll clean up everything, returning my materials and journals to their usual safe locations. As I prepare to welcome the family home, the mini-retreat will be finished. So mote it be! |

And here is that same daylong plan in a more "skeletal," pared-down version:

Call to adventure:	Learn more about working with herbs
Type of focus:	Practice, testing, and trial
Magickal goals:	Make and use at least three different infusions with fresh and dried herbs. Work with tools and do some studying.
Time:	8:30–4:30 Monday
Place:	Kitchen and dining room
Timing details:	Monday— new beginnings
Magickal activities:	Making infusions, tea leaf reading
Spiritual activities:	Ritual shower, blessings
Mundane activities:	Lunch and walk
Creating mood:	Ginger candle, CD

Embracing silence, slowness, and a quiet pace:	No TV, no cell phone
Food:	Simple lunch and snack; no cooking
Materials needed:	Herbs, infusion materials, guidebooks, paper and pencil
Departure (more on this in chapter 8):	After everyone leaves
Schedule:	Morning: Work with infusions, take notes, journal Lunch and walk Afternoon: More infusion work; start formulary; flash cards
Return (more on this in chapter 9):	Clean-up, journal, reflect

Plan for an Overnight Retreat:

Here is the same "Herbology 101" plan yet again, only this time it's designed to fill an overnight and takes place in a different location. This will begin with the same content as the daylong retreat, but will expand to include use of additional herbal techniques, including perhaps the creation of creams and balms and essential oils.

Call to adventure:	Learn more about working with herbs; practice with infusions and with simple recipes for creams and lip balms. Begin my own formulary.
Type of focus:	Practice, testing, and trial
Magickal goals:	Make and use at least three different infusions with fresh and dried herbs. Make one cream and one lip balm. Work with tools and do some studying. Begin developing my personal herbal formulary.
Time:	5:00 p.m. Friday to 8:00 p.m. Saturday, June 3
Place:	Myrna's beach cabin
Timing details:	Planned around a full moon night
Magickal activities:	Making herbal preparations; tea leaf reading; full moon ritual with charging of water and tools

Spiritual activities:	Cleansing shower, ritual of beginning, blessings, full moon ritual, ritual of leaving
Mundane activities:	Meals, morning walk
Creating mood:	Fire in fireplace, candles (in Mason jars?), music
Embracing silence, slowness, and a quiet pace:	No TV, radio, cell service, or Internet
Food:	Simple dinner; sumptuous brunch; early supper on Saturday; snack before heading home. Lots of tea, water; fruit for snacks.
Materials needed:	Herbs, preparation tools and materials, guidebooks, paper and pencil, laptop, ritual kit, jar for moon water, camera
Departure (more on this in chapter 8):	Prepare dinner for family; once they're home, get them settled and then depart. As I step over the front-door threshold, I'll understand that I am entering my retreat space. So mote it be!
Schedule:	Friday evening: Arrive at cabin; start fire and get it warmed up. Take a cleansing shower and do a quick ritual of beginning, announcing my intentions. Before bed, conduct a full moon ritual (outdoors if possible). Leave water and herb tools to charge overnight in the moonlight. Early morning: Cup of tea, morning walk (look for day sign). Bring in moon water and tools. Ground, center. Work on crafting infusions. Read tea leaves after each one. Record results. Photos as needed. Late morning: Big breakfast! Blessing over food. Journal about morning activities. Midday to early afternoon: Create cream and lip balm. Begin work on herbal formulary: outline first, then sketch out first entries. Late afternoon: Another quick walk. Light dinner w/ blessing. Journal on events of the day. Gather up materials, clean up cabin. Leave thank-you note. Carry out ritual of leaving. Depart for home.
Return (more on this in chapter 9):	Stop to get ice cream for family. Once home, put materials away. Shower. Return to the mundane.

Plan for a Long Retreat

Here's the big kahuna . . . Our plan for an herbal-focused retreat now morphs into a long weekend that begins on Friday afternoon and extends through Monday evening. This includes the same content as the overnight retreat but finds the retreater practicing additional techniques, doing more focused study, and taking a wildcrafting outing, where she'll practice ethical plant gathering and learn to press, dry, and store herbs. This retreat will also include some loosely scheduled time aimed purely at relaxation.

Call to adventure:	Learn more about working with herbs; practice with infusions and with simple recipes for creams and lip balms. Make a dream pillow and an herbal charm. Go wildcrafting! Woo hoo! Prepare herbs for drying. Begin my own formulary.
Type of focus:	Practice, testing, and trial + escape
Magickal goals:	Make and use at least five different infusions with fresh and dried herbs. Make one cream and one lip balm. Work with tools and do some studying. Begin developing my personal herbal formulary. Go wildcrafting. Practice plant ID, and collect and prepare at least one plant.
Time:	3:00 p.m. Friday to 8:00 p.m. Monday, August 12.
Place:	Yurt at the local state park, near the beach. Must cook outdoors. Propane-heated. Showers at nearby campground.
Timing details:	Full moon on Friday
Magickal activities:	Making herbal preparations; tea leaf reading; full moon ritual with charging of water and tools
Spiritual activities:	Cleansing shower before leaving home, ritual of beginning upon reaching yurt, blessings, full moon ritual, ritual of leaving
Mundane activities:	Meals, walks, beachcombing, plus an art gallery afternoon (fun!). Check regulations on wildcrafting in area.
Creating mood:	Fire in fireplace, candles, music
Embracing silence, slowness, and a quiet pace:	No TV, radio, or Internet. Cell service available but phone will be off. Will check messages A.M. and P.M.

Food: Friday	Friday: Fast food meal en route; apple for evening snack
Food: Saturday	Saturday breakfast: Coffee, oatmeal Saturday lunch: Sandwich, fruit, chips Saturday afternoon snack: Cookies and milk Saturday dinner: Spaghetti (made ahead) Saturday evening: Herbal tea (no caffeine!), cookies
Food: Sunday	Sunday breakfast: Coffee, oatmeal Sunday lunch: Sandwich, fruit, chips Sunday (early) dinner: Dine out at seafood restaurant in town! Sunday evening: Dessert (take-out from restaurant dinner)
Food: Monday	Monday morning: Coffee or tea Monday mid-morning: Into town for brunch (get chowder for lunch, too) Monday late afternoon: Clam chowder (take-out from town) Before heading home: Snack on whatever's left Also: Lots of tea, water, fresh fruit; marshmallows for campfire ☺
Materials needed:	Herbs, preparation tools and materials, guidebooks; paper and pencil; laptop; ritual kit; jar for moon water; camera; camp stove with propane and matches; cooking gear; tableware; sleeping bag and pillow; personal gear; quarters for shower; towels; battery-powered lantern; flashlight; "for pleasure" book; firewood; water jug; unused telephone book; plant shears; scraps of fabric, swing kit.
Departure (more on this in chapter 8):	Arrange after-school pick-up for kids. Depart home by 3 p.m. As I step over the front-door threshold, I'll understand that I am entering my retreat "other" space. So mote it be!
Schedule: Friday	Evening: Arrive at yurt; pause mindfully upon entering yurt. Start propane heater and get the space warmed up. Carry out a ritual of beginning, announcing my intentions for the retreat. Bless the space with herbs or salt. Later evening: Full moon ritual (outdoors and with campfire if possible). Leave water and herb tools to charge overnight in the moonlight. Lay out materials for tomorrow's work. Read at bedtime.

Schedule: Saturday	Morning: Quick morning walk (look for day sign). Bring in moon water and tools. Have breakfast*. Ground, center. Work on crafting infusions. Read tea leaves after each one. Record results. Photos as needed. Journal before lunch.
	(*All meals will be preceded by hand washing and a blessing over food.)
	Early afternoon: Have lunch. More work with infusions, both hot and cold. Begin work on herbal formulary: outline first, then sketch out first entries.
	Mid-afternoon: Beachcombing; watch for natural augurs; look for holey stones, sea glass, or other special materials. Collect sand for later ritual use.
	Later afternoon: Begin work on herbal formulary. Journal on events of the day. Gather up materials, clean up yurt. Prepare dinner.
	Evening: Campfire outdoors if weather permits. Use herbs (selected per magickal correspondence), beach grass, and fabric to sew a dream pillow.
	Bedtime: Tuck the dream pillow under my own pillow; meditate briefly on the dreams I hope to have.
Schedule: Sunday	Morning: Immediately upon waking, journal about any dream results. Shower and breakfast. Head out on a wildcrafting outing. Goals: (1) at least three cuttings to identify and press; (2) plant ID practice. Take photos for formulary. Upon arriving home, rinse collected specimens and lay out to air-dry.
	Midday: Have lunch. Journal about wildcrafting outing. Settle in for work on herbal formulary. Arrange collected specimens (they should be mostly dried) in the pages of the phone book and weight with stones.
	Mid-afternoon: Into town for town/gallery (and bookstore!) visits; 4 p.m.-ish dinner at local restaurant. (Don't forget take-out dessert.)
	Early evening: Continue work on herbal formulary. Journal on events of the day. Gather up materials, tidy up yurt.

Schedule: Sunday continued	*Evening: Campfire outdoors if weather permits. Enjoy special dessert. Use herbs, beach treasures, beach sand, cold ashes from edge of fire pit, and fabric to sew a small charm or amulet. Perhaps try some fire-scrying or meditation. Consider my retreat so far: what have I learned? Come in and journal, then to bed.*
Schedule: Monday	*Morning: Carry a cup of coffee or tea along for a relaxing morning walk on the beach (look for day sign). Head into town for breakfast and any other stops needed. Pick up chowder for lunch.* *Later morning: Prepare at least one cream and one balm. Record recipes and journal re: results.* *Early afternoon: Lunch. (Chowder! Yum!) Finish any work with creams and balms if needed. Continue work on herbal formulary.* *Later afternoon: Gather up materials, clean up yurt. Pack car. Collect sample of ashes from the fire pit to keep for ritual purposes.* *Early evening: Reflective journal entry about the retreat experience. Carry out ritual of leaving. Depart for home.*
Return (more on this in chapter 9):	*Stop to get ice cream for family. Once home, unpack and put materials away. Shower. Return to the mundane.*

Look What's Coming!

In each of the "focus" chapters (chapters 10–21), I'll suggest a number of activities and magickal ideas for each focus and will present several ready-to-use ideas and one complete retreat outline. You may use any of these "as is" or you may dip in and out, selecting specific ideas as desired and using them to design your own retreat plan.

But now, it's time. Review your notes from the previous chapters and craft your retreat from beginning to end. You'll find one template on the pages that follow and additional blank templates in Appendix B at the back of the book.

Template for Retreat Planning

Call to adventure:	
Type of Focus	
Magickal goals:	
Time:	
Place:	
Timing details:	
Magickal activities:	
Spiritual activities:	
Mundane activities:	
Creating mood:	
Embracing silence, slowness, and a quiet pace:	

Food:	
Materials needed:	
Departure:	
Schedule:	

Schedule continued:	
Return:	

Tasks for Chapter 7

1. What do you think of the sample retreats in this chapter? How did they resonate with you?

_____

_____

_____

_____

2. Which retreat example do you think suits you best? Why? How did you incorporate this into your plan?

_____

_____

_____

_____

3. Now that you've begun to create a retreat plan, which part or parts of it are you happiest with? Which part or parts still need more work? Make a plan for continued work . . .

_____

_____

_____

_____

Notes

_____

_____

_____

_____

Chapter Eight

Departure and Initiation

Whatever you think you can do or believe you can do, begin it.
Action has magic, grace, and power in it.

—JOHANN WOLFGANG VON GOETHE

The retreat draws closer. You have a written plan and you've gathered intention. You've used the hero's journey metaphor as a way not only to enrich your own experience but to forge connection with your ancestral and modern "others" through shared experience. It's time now for your journey to begin!

Preparing for Departure

Take care of the mundane details first—packing food, materials, and so on. Remember your trip plan: make sure that at least one other person knows where you'll be, how you're traveling, how to reach you, and when to expect you back—these points are nothing less than basic safety.

Once the mundane is cared for, turn to your magickal preparations. Purification is an important part of all magickal undertakings, and I suggest that you bathe or shower just before the retreat begins. Draw a deep tub of water (or turn on a steamy shower) and use a fresh bar of soap—frankincense or juniper soaps are excellent for ritual purification. Wash carefully, rinse, and then totally immerse yourself. As you do, imagine your skin and self being washed clean. Envision yourself as a fresh, blank slate, ready for whatever the coming experience has to teach you.

Towel dry, applying lotion or powder and imagining a protective shield taking shape around you. Dress comfortably in fresh, clean clothes that are loose and cozy. If desired, wear magickal regalia, such as robes, tabard, or shawl. Magickal jewelry may also be an important part of your retreat.

Mindfulness

Go back to chapter 6 and reread the content about mindfulness. This is so very important: your ability to be present in the moment, undistracted, is probably more critical than anything else in making your retreat as success. Listen. Ground. Observe. Consider. Be open to guidance. Be aware, focused, and "present." This is your retreat, and you want to experience every second.

Follow the Schedule, But…

Stay flexible. One of my past mentors taught me to be "flegid": flexible, but rigid. Following a schedule will help you finish your projects and realize the specific goals you've set for your retreat. But don't be so locked in to the schedule that you forget why you're there—i.e., to have a rewarding, inspiring experience. If some wonderful opportunity presents itself, don't be afraid to shift gears, let go of the schedule, and go after it. That's part of the fun of the retreat, after all—the joy, the spontaneity, and the discovery. The *possibility.*

Journaling

Return to chapter 3 and scan over my comments about journaling. As you reviewed the sample retreats in the previous sections, you probably noticed a recurring theme in all of them: journaling. Even if you aren't a regular journal user, I encourage you to put the practice into play for your retreat. Journaling is essential for capturing insights and ideas as well as writing down processes that you hope to repeat. Plan time in your retreat for writing down your progress.

Observation

The word *observe* comes from a Latin root meaning "to watch," and to observe is to become more aware through careful and directed attention. Observation means taking that careful attention and using it to notice or record various occurrences or phenomena. If you're observant, you're alert and quick to perceive or notice things.

Observation doesn't come naturally to many of us. In our busy everyday lives, we're usually moving too fast. We tend to focus on our immediate sphere and whatever we're concerned with at the moment, and we often aren't really aware of the complex world moving around us. Fortunately, the skills of observation—like all magickal skills—can be practiced, and learned.

At its core, good observation is all about two things: patience and repetition. If you want to become a good observer, you must be willing to spend the time and patience to do so. A good way to practice is to sit motionless and silent in a natural area, waiting to see and hear what happens around you. As the wildlife becomes accustomed to your presence, you'll begin to see more activity around you. As for repetition, in order to understand the behavior of magick, the natural world, or any organic process, you must observe, process what you've seen, and then observe again, allowing your knowledge base to build enough to see patterns and make informed deductions.

As you practice observation, you'll find yourself looking at the magickal and mundane worlds with renewed curiosity and understanding, and your work will take on new richness. Throughout your retreat, keep your senses alert and your observational powers sharp. Watch for day signs, augurs, messages, and unusual or unexpected occurrences. When something unexpected appears in your view, don't brush it aside: consider its meaning and reflect on what it's trying to tell you. Journal about the event so you can go back and reflect on it later; you'll be surprised at how much meaning most of these so-called "random occurrences" really have.

Facing Challenges

Joseph Campbell's quest model includes a section where the hero-to-be is tempted away from the path. Like Campbell's hero, you'll undoubtedly face a number of challenges or tests on your journey—some might even pop up before you depart. Meet each one head on and without fear, working through the possible approaches and outcomes and considering the skills and resources you have at hand. Then move forward, making adjustments as needed. Your testing may be part of an initiation: keep this in mind as you face each challenge. Once the test or obstacle is vanquished, make a journal entry describing how you dealt with it. Include the concrete details, but you should also write about your mental and magickal success—i.e., the confidence and skill with which you met the challenge as well as the eventual outcome.

Divine Intervention

If you work with guardians, deities, patrons, spirit guides, totems, or any other sort of magickal mentor, you may certainly speak with or appeal to them throughout your retreat. For that matter, they may show up and decide to address you directly. Campbell would call this a meeting or intervention with the God or Goddess, and it can be a powerful adjunct to your retreat.

Remember, though: this is *your* journey. Personal growth only comes when we meet and overcome new challenges. Seek advice if needed, but have the courage to proceed on your own, too. Sense your growing strength as you meet and conquer each hurdle, and rejoice, knowing that each step taken strengthens you for whatever waits around the next corner.

Adding Ritual

Campbell's journey model is framed on both ends by the mention of a threshold: the hero crosses the threshold on the way out and crosses it again on the way back home. Your retreat should likewise have "bookends"; that is, it should begin and end with some sort of ritual or, at the very least, a mindful pause and awareness of the threshold, dedication to your goals, or both. These actions create a time container that transports you and your experiences outside of the mundane and emphasizes your entry into the magickal realm of liminal space. It sets the mood of importance and will give you that encompassing feeling of truly beginning and finishing a journey.

Begin your retreat mindfully, and with intention—remember the "stretching forward" we spoke of earlier? Stop for a moment and be aware of your movement into a new place. Focus on your intentions. Visualize yourself not simply thinking about but actually achieving your goals. You could offer a prayer, meditate, work a magickal charm, or carry out ritual as well.

Step over the threshold.

And so it begins . . .

Tasks for Chapter 8

Here are some final questions . . .

1. What details do you still have to iron out before you depart? What needs to be finished before your retreat?

_____

_____

_____

_____

2. What are you most looking forward to on your retreat?

_____

_____

_____

_____

3. What tests do you think you may face along the "road of trials"?

_____

_____

_____

_____

4. Is there anything you're concerned about? How can you resolve your concerns before you begin?

_____

_____

_____

_____

5. Will you undergo some form of initiation? Describe it.

_____

_____

_____

_____

6. What single word best describes your emotions as you prepare to cross the threshold?

_____

_____

_____

_____

Notes and Ideas:

_____

_____

_____

_____

Suggested Resources for This Chapter

Campbell, Joseph. *The Hero with a Thousand Faces.* New World Library, 2008. (*Campbell's seminal writing on the monomyth and the hero's journey.*)

Dalai Lama (His Holiness the). *365: Daily Advice from the Heart.* ThorsonElement, 2001. (*A wonderful little book of daily meditations.*)

Henes, Donna. *Celestially Auspicious Occasions: Seasons, Cycles, & Celebrations.* Perigee, 1996.

Return

The gem cannot be polished without friction, nor man perfected without trials.

—CHINESE PROVERB

Great things are not done by impulse,
but by a series of small things brought together.

—VINCENT VAN GOGH

Long is the road from conception to completion.

—MOLIÈRE

Before this distinguished assembly and the world, the bells today proclaim
the joyous tidings of the completion of this quietly soaring tower.

—EARL WARREN

It is not the mountain we conquer, but ourselves.

—SIR EDMUND HILLARY

Once the quest has been completed but a few simple tasks remain . . .

Crossing the Return Threshold

Once you step back across the home threshold, your retreat will be complete. You planned the details, faced challenges, and had a wonderful and useful experience. You may not have wanted to return to reality, and perhaps your return was nudged by Joseph Campbell's ideas of magickal intervention or flight. Maybe you were only willing to return to the daily grind because you'd already begun thinking about and planning your next retreat. In any case, you're back home again, and it's likely that the world looks a little different. This reflects your new knowledge, skills, and perhaps even the results of a rite of passage or initiation. You've journeyed, you've returned, and you now have access to two worlds.

Apotheosis

One of the most important parts of Campbell's journey is the idea of the seeker's apotheosis—i.e., becoming strong, powerful, and a force to be reckoned with. In age-old mythology, apotheosis meant becoming god-like, and this was something that ancient humans aspired to. While you may not have become god- or goddess-like, you have completed your retreat, meaning you've surmounted the testing, met your goals, and found your way back. Make sure to reflect back on your retreat. Consider those moments when you felt a calm certainty about what you were doing—moments when you felt capable, sure, and confident. Think about the points at which you thought, "Yes—I can do this," or, "Wow . . . This is really wonderful." Take time to journal about these discoveries, for they are at the very heart of the retreat experience. When did they happen? What prompted them? How did you feel at that very moment?

The Ultimate Boon: Receiving the Gifts

In the traditional hero's journey, the quest ends with the receiving of a boon. The modern meaning of the word *boon* is a tool or object that is useful or beneficial. Interestingly, the arcane meaning of the term references the Latin *bonus*, which meant "good fellow" or, in the context of those times, a good drinking companion!

But you'll want more than a drinking buddy here. All quests end with some sort of boon, often a symbolic reaping in the form of new knowledge and skills. Many of the old quests had a literal prize at the center—like the Holy Grail or the Golden Fleece. Quite a few modern quests have some sort of tangible result as well, as in the diploma given to the college graduate (and yes, college is definitely a hero's journey).

Your boon may come in the form of knowledge, abilities, a new name, increased status or awareness, fresh insights, renewed understanding, or something else. If you choose, you may also create a tangible item to remind you of your completion of the journey. If you do this, it will serve as a powerful symbol and recollection of what you've done; it may also tie you—via sympathetic magick—to the experience.

And by the way: I suggest you pick up a small stone from your retreat location. Stones carry ancient place-memories, and a stone will become a powerful memento and talisman to mark your experience. If your retreat takes you to the ocean, a seashell, agate, or piece of sea glass will serve nicely.

Honoring the Experience and Accepting the Responsibilities

Now, standing at the end of your retreat, you're no doubt considering the experience and thinking about what happened and where you have ended up. A period of self-evaluation awaits, but first, while the experience is still fresh, stop and honor the experience. With every completed journey come both gifts and responsibilities, and you should consider how to apply these to your own path as well as considering how they impact others.

Should You Talk About It?

Many magick users follow the dictum of not talking about their magickal works for some time after the spells or ritual are enacted. They believe that talking about them dilutes the action and may interfere with the results. You may wish to follow this guide in terms of your retreat. Keep in mind that you've just completed a rather powerful—and hopefully meaningful—experience, and by remaining silent for a time, you hold the power within, keeping it for yourself and continuing to reap additional benefits and insights.

When you arrive home after the retreat, I would suggest keeping silent about the event and the details. Don't talk about the retreat to other people, but do "talk" to your journal, capturing memories, feelings, discoveries, etc. After a week or two have passed, it could be time to discuss the specifics with your mentor, family, or magickal friends. Of course, your mileage may vary, and how you handle this is up to you. If talking about it right away seems right to you, go for it.

Sharing Your Gifts

Consider how you, as a "returned" and newly wise seeker, may now become teacher or mentor for others in turn. You now understand Campbell's "freedom to live." You know that you're capable of stepping back and forth between daily mundane space and liminal/other space, and you have the power and insight to choose when and how to move between them. With that knowledge comes an implied obligation.

One of my mentors taught me this mantra: "*Each one, see one, do one, teach one.*" In other words, we're taught, we learn, and then we teach someone else. How can you take your newly found skills and ideas and share them with someone else? The continuum between teacher and student is one of the thriving magickal cycles that spins through our cosmos, adding to the flow of energy. Teaching an activity to another person also cements the learning in one's own mind and deepens the experience. Perhaps you'll share your experiences through an online blog, an in-person presentation to your magickal group, or with your own students or initiates. I'd love to hear from you, too. See chapter 22 for more information on that.

Giving Thanks

I suggest you give thanks to and honor those who have helped you along the path. Consider sending a teacher-mentor a simple thank-you card or gift her with some sort of magickal item of enduring significance. Thank your friends, family, and magickal community, too, for their support of your magickal path. As suggested earlier in the book, if your retreat took you some distance away from your family, it's always fun to bring them back a little gift or token.

Celebration!

In traditional cultures past and present, great celebrations and feasts are often held for the person who has surmounted an obstacle, completed a rite of passage, or returned from a vision quest or retreat. You should likewise plan to celebrate your accomplishment. Perhaps you'll plan a special meal to enjoy after your retreat is over, whether alone or with friends, covenmates, your mentor, or others. Include a toast with champagne, wine, or mead if that suits you.

I'd also encourage you to make a lasting piece of garb, regalia, or some other "relic" to mark your journey in a tangible way. You could purchase a piece of jewelry or some sort of magickal implement: for instance, a new pen, a special journal, or an altarpiece. Make it special, and guard it as the treasure it is.

In Campbell's journey, the returning hero is now the master of two worlds. She has seen both sides and understands that she has the skills to do well in either position, freeing her up to make an informed decision about where she most *wants* to be. She values the thrill and challenge of the road, but she's quite happy to be back home among friends, family, and familiar surroundings. Of course, that doesn't mean she isn't already thinking about the next great adventure.

What's Next?

In chapters 10–21, you'll read through ideas for a number of different types of retreats. If something catches your eye as you read, circle it or put a star or something next to it; that way, you'll be able to find it again easily. Happy reading!

Tasks for Chapter 9

Evaluation is a critical part of any retreat activity. Having experienced one retreat, it's very likely you'll plan others, and thinking through what did or didn't work—as well as what you'd do the same or differently next time—can be a big help in making future plans. For this chapter's tasks, please ask yourself these questions and write answers in your journal:

1. What was the best part of the experience? What did you enjoy most?

_____

_____

_____

_____

2. What worked well?

_____

_____

_____

_____

3. What worked but didn't work smoothly?

_____

_____

_____

_____

4. What didn't work at all?

_____

_____

_____

_____

5. What would you do differently next time?

_____

_____

_____

_____

6. What would you do *more* of next time?

_____

_____

_____

_____

7. If you were to plan another retreat, what new ideas do you have? What would you focus on?

_____

_____

_____

_____

8. If a friend was planning a retreat and you could give him or her one piece of
advice, what would it be?

_____

_____

_____

_____

Notes and Ideas

_____

_____

_____

_____

Suggested Resources for This Chapter

Henes, Donna. *Celestially Auspicious Occasions: Seasons, Cycles, & Celebrations.* Perigee, 1996.

Mosley, Ivo, ed. *Earth Poems: Poems from Around the World to Honor the Earth.* HarperSanFrancisco, 1996.

Roberts, Elizabeth, and Elias Amidon, eds. *Life Prayers: 365 Prayers, Blessings, and Affirmations to Celebrate the Human Journey.* HarperSanFrancisco, 1996.

Serith, Ceisiwr. *A Book of Pagan Prayer.* Weiser, 2002. (*A lovely collection of Pagan-oriented prayers and blessings for all occasions from the casual to the celebratory.*)

Zell-Ravenheart, Oberon, and Morning Glory Zell-Ravenheart. *Creating Circles and Ceremonies: Rituals for All Seasons and Reasons.* New Page Books, 2006.

Part IV

Individual
Retreat Plans

It is good to have an end to journey toward,
but it is the journey that matters in the end.

—URSULA K. LE GUIN

Chapter Ten

Magickal Skills Focus

Magickal skills are those aspects that we regard as traditional or essential parts of magickal practice. Think of them as "Magick 101," but also realize that deep expression of these practices can become an especially dense, rich part of one's magickal or spiritual life.

Ideas for a retreat focused on magickal skills

- Build or renew an altar shrine space. This could be indoor or outdoors.
- Make miniature or portable altars. Include small candles, miniature statuary, matches, a charcoal tablet or two, a tiny drinking vessel, or the like. Small tins are perfect for this—in my group, we call these Altoid altars. Another friend keeps her mini-altar in a small bag and calls it her Porta-Pagan.
- Work with stone, gem, and/or crystal magicks.
- Practice candle magicks.
- Work with magickal spells, charms, or blessings. Consider magickal workings that will be coming up in the near future or work with ongoing needs, such as house blessings or safe travel charms. Spend a day working with materials to construct a set of ready-to-use magickal items.

- Work with amulets and talismans. An amulet is a piece of jewelry, a small pouch, or some other object felt to protect again harm or danger. A talisman is similar, but it works more like a battery, drawing positive intentional magick in toward the user and providing protection.

- Study a specific magickal practice, such as cord and knot magick, sympathetic magick, hex craft, weather working, or puppetry.

- Explore magickal ethics. Write your own Code of Magickal Practice and dedicate yourself to it.

- Study and memorize an important piece of magickal writing—e.g., the (complete) Wiccan Rede, the Charge of the Goddess, the Emerald Tablet. Finish by writing it into your magickal journal or Book of Shadows.

- Study, memorize, and/or work with magickal correspondences or symbols.

Sample retreat ideas

1. **Learn about candle work**. Read and study about candle craft. Make two or more candles, using a method of choice and working with color, scent, and possibly "hard" additions like crystals or herbs. Dress or anoint the finished candles and, if possible, use them for a magickal ritual or purpose. Take careful journal notes, detailing your actions, recipes, and so on.

2. **Develop your own tables or lists of correspondences.** Using resource materials, create a detailed table of correspondences for each of the four cardinal elements. Enter the results into your magickal journal. You might also use index cards to make a set of flash cards using the correspondences.

3. **Develop tables or lists of specific correspondences for a set purpose.** Determine one or two types of spells, charms, or other magickal practices that you'd like to work with. For example, imagine you wanted to (a) craft a love spell and (b) create a set of stones to support memory and wisdom. Using resource materials, create a detailed table of correspondences for each of the practices you've selected. Enter the results into your magickal journal. Use index cards to make a set of flash cards using the correspondences.

4. **Consider your views on magickal ethics**. Begin by writing down your own preliminary ideas about magickal ethics. How do you define ethical magickal

practices? What are safe, sensible guidelines? Why is ethical practice important? Do some research on magickal ethics—the Web is a good place to find a wide view of different opinions. Once you've done this, write your own Code of Magickal Practice. Enter it into your magickal journal. Sign and date it. Carry out a ritual in which you bind yourself to this Code. Resolve to reread and, if needed, revise the Code every few months. You could develop a ritual practice that involves you rededicating yourself to the Code at intervals.

5. **Craft and indoor altar space**. Determine a location for an indoor altar. Devote your retreat time to cleansing and preparing the site and to installing an altar. You could also devote time to preparing specific items for the altar: for example, painting a piece of statuary or a panticle (a work surface used on an altar), grinding incense, or polishing stones. Finish, of course, with a ritual or a bit of spellwork conducted at your brand-new altar.

Sample overnight retreat for work with stones and crystals

Call to adventure:	I feel drawn to stones and would like to study them and learn more about their uses.
Type of focus:	Practice, testing, and trial
Magickal goals:	Build an initial collection of 10 stones or crystals. Study each stone and read/research, too. Create a journal page for each and a storage pouch. Be more ready to use stones in magickal practice.
Time:	Noon Saturday to 5:00 p.m. Sunday
Place:	B&B at Cannon Beach (has microwave)
Timing details:	Extra-low tide on Saturday morning
Magickal activities:	Stone/crystal study; cleanse stones and charge in the beach sun; create a bag of holding for storage; work in magickal journal
Spiritual activities:	Charm for safe travel, blessings over food, ritual of leaving.
Mundane activities:	Meals, morning beachcombing; might check a couple of galleries or bookstores in town on Sunday afternoon.
Creating mood:	Candles, music

Embracing silence, slowness, and a quiet pace:	No TV, radio, cell service, or Internet. Will bring iPad for music.
Food:	Sub sandwich on the way out of town Saturday; dinner in town on Saturday night; breakfast at B&B on Sunday; late lunch en route home. Lots of tea, water; fruit for snacks.
Materials needed:	Stones (will stop at rock shop before leaving town and pick out 10 specimens that call to me); gem and mineral books; fabric and sewing notions for bag of holding; journal, pens, and pencils; candles, jars, and matches; empty bottle for sea water; book for pleasure reading; camera.
Departure:	As I step into the car, I'll officially enter retreat space. So mote it be!
Schedule:	Saturday noon: Stop at rock shop and pick up stones and crystals. Drive to beach and check into B&B by 3 p.m. Settle in and set up work area. Wash stones, pat dry, and set out on the work space. Begin reading about each one. Saturday evening: Drive into town for early dinner. Get a take-out dessert or snack. Return to B&B. Take a cleansing bath and do a quick ritual of beginning, announcing my intentions. Put jammies on and brew a cup of tea. Continue work with stones. Hold each one and meditate on it, making notes about any impressions received. Read/research. Begin a journal page for each stone, noting magickal and mundane attributes and observations. Cut out and sew a simple drawstring bag to hold stones. Late evening: Set stones in window to greet the rising sun (or in moonlight, if available). Enjoy dessert (blessing over food)! Offer a prayer before bed. Read, sleep.

Schedule: continued	Sunday morning: B&B breakfast. Morning beachcombing (take jar!). Look for day sign and comb for agates, shells, and holey stones. Take photos. Collect a jar of sea water. Remove shoes and stand in Mother Ocean's waters, giving thanks. Return to B&B. Wash newly found objects. Meditate, asking for insight and inspiration. Continue work with studying and journaling. Mid-afternoon: Pack up. Check out of B&B. Do a ritual of leaving and again ask for safe travel. Leave thank-you note. Stop at galleries and bookstores in town. Depart for home, grabbing lunch en route.
Return:	Greet family. Unpack, returning stones to a safe place where they won't be touched by others. Journal about the experience.

Notes and Ideas

Suggested Resources for This Chapter

Cunningham, Scott. *Cunningham's Encyclopedia of Crystal, Gem, and Metal Magick.* Llewellyn, 1998.

———. *The Complete Book of Incense, Oils, and Brews.* Llewellyn, 2002.

Pellant, Chris. *Rocks and Minerals (Smithsonian Handbook).* DK Adult, 2002.

Telesco, Patricia. *Exploring Candle Magick.* Career, 2008.

Zell-Ravenheart, Oberon. *Companion for the Apprentice Wizard.* New Page Books, 2004. (*A detail-packed sequel to Zell-Ravenheart's* Grimoire.)

———. *Grimoire for the Apprentice Wizard.* New Page Books, 2004. (*This book, which has been described as a "Boy Scout Handbook for magick users," is rich with "how-tos" and tables of correspondences, planetary hours, rituals, spellwork, and the like.*)

Chapter Eleven

Pathwork Focus

Pathwork refers to one's alliance with a specific magickal or spiritual path or tradition. Whether you are Druid, Pagan, Faery, or Chaos mage, focusing on your tradition may provide you with a wonderful and rewarding retreat focus.

Ideas for a retreat focused on pathwork

1. Study and/or explore a defined magickal craft or tradition.

    - Alchemy
    - Druidism
    - Faery
    - Pagan tradition as a modern movement
    - Shamanism
    - Wicca (one or more of the types)
    - Other paths

2. Study mythology or folklore, or take a wider approach to these subjects: e.g., undertake an in-depth study of Joseph Campbell's "monomyth" or *The Hero*

with a Thousand Faces, delve into academic folklore structures, study Carl Jung's writings.

3. Complete steps or stages in a magickal study or discipline.

4. Design a course of self-study.

5. Plan a course of study or apprenticeship for others, such as a coven or a group of students.

6. Plan and practice your role in a magickal event: e.g., a Pagan Pride day or a workshop.

7. Practice stage magic—"magic without the *k*."

Sample retreat ideas

1. **Perform "comparative studies."** Learn more about a magickal discipline by digging into and reading information from a variety of "experts" in the area. For example, if exploring Wicca, look into work by Raymond Buckland, Starhawk, Gerald Gardner, and the modern WitchSchool. If exploring Druidism, compare Celtic reconstructionist, modern eclectic, and Neo-Pagan Druid traditions.

2. **Study more about Joseph Campbell**. Explore Campbell's work and consider how it applies to all types of magickal practice and exploration. You might compare your own magickal path against his classical "hero's journey" model (see also chapter 2 in this book), as well as using the same model to make plans for your own path in the months and years to come.

3. **Work on developing a class or course of training.** If you are in charge of educating students, fosterlings, or apprentices, use your retreat time to map out a course of study, develop a curriculum, write a class, etc.

4. **Practice stage magic.** Study the fine art of conjury. Arm yourself with instructional materials, YouTube videos, and the like, and practice developing skills and special effects. Make a plan to share your new skills with others.

Sample one-day retreat for developing a course of self-study aimed at personal growth

Call to adventure:	I consider myself a Pagan, but I realize I don't know much about how the movement started. I feel a need to know more about these magickal roots.
Type of focus:	Sabbatical
Magickal goals:	Explore two seminal books on Paganism in the US: Adler's "Drawing Down the Moon" and Zell-Ravenheart's "Green Egg Omelette." Develop a course of self-study that incorporates the two books and involves writing reflective essays as each section is completed.
Time:	All day Wednesday, while the house is empty.
Place:	Home: dining room. Spread out everything on the table.
Timing details:	Wednesday is ideal for work involving wisdom, creativity, and divination.
Magickal activities:	Focused study; work with magickal journal; make bookmarks
Spiritual activities:	Begin with brief candle-lighting ritual at the altar, asking for mental clarity and inspiration.
Mundane activities:	Lunch
Creating mood:	Celtic music in the background.
Embracing silence, slowness, and a quiet pace:	TV off; I will avoid the Internet unless I need to cross-check facts.
Food:	Yummy sandwich for lunch, with my favorite kettle chips. (Treat!) Brew peppermint-thyme tea for mental clarity.
Materials needed:	Books, paper, pen, laptop (magickal journal is kept there), calendar, bookmark fabric, scissors, herbs for tea
Departure:	Brief opening ritual at altar. Perhaps wear magickal shawl. Wash hands before beginning to show entry into sacred workspace.

Schedule:	*Wednesday morning: As soon as John leaves for work, settle in and begin. Start by listing the chapters for each book, looking for obvious similarities. List page counts for each section. Begin reading: skim first 1-2 pages of each section to get a "feel," taking notes with pen & paper.*
	Noon-ish: Pause for lunch.
	Afternoon: Finish the skim-reading. Develop a working plan for moving through and finishing the books, moving back and forth from one to another. Referring to calendar, create a reading schedule: aim for about 200 pages per week. Develop a plan to journal or even write a reflective essay following completion of each section. Perhaps arrange to share these with a mentor. Perhaps also think of ways to put into play whatever was learned.
	Late afternoon: Enter results into the magickal journal. Cut out bookmarks and place on altar to "charge." Spend any remaining time working on initial reading assignment.
Return:	*Put everything away. Return to altar and carry out a brief closing ritual.*

Notes and Ideas

_____

_____

_____

_____

Suggested Resources for This Chapter

Adler, Margo. *Drawing Down the Moon: Witches, Druids, Goddess-Worshippers, and Other Pagans in America.* Penguin, 2006.

Bonewits, Isaac, and Philip Carr-Gomm. *Bonewits' Essential Guide to Druidism.* Citadel, 2006.

Brunvand, Jan. *The Study of American Folklore, 4th edition.* Norton, 1998.

Buckland, Raymond. *Buckland's Complete Book of Witchcraft.* Llewellyn, 2002. (*A look at Gardnerian-influenced Wicca for the beginner.*)

Campbell, Joseph. *The Hero with a Thousand Faces.* New World Library, 2008. (*Campbell's seminal writing on the monomyth and the hero's journey.*)

Campbell, Joseph, and Bill Moyers. *The Power of Myth.* Anchor, 1991. (*Campbell's work on the importance of mythos through world cultures.*)

Jung, C. G. *The Red Book.* Norton, 2009.

Starhawk. *The Spiral Dance: A Rebirth of the Ancient Religion of the Goddess, 20th Anniversary Edition.* HarperOne, 1999.

Zell-Ravenheart, Oberon. *Green Egg Omelette: An Anthology of Art and Articles from the Legendary Pagan Journal.* New Page Books, 2008.

Chapter Twelve

Home Arts Focus

Home arts are those specific "homey" practices that support home and hearth—the kinds of activities we might do in a kitchen or sewing room. Think of these as the kinds of domestic arts a "hedge witch" might spend time doing. Needlework and kitchen magick are important parts of this focus.

Ideas for a retreat focused on home arts

Work with traditional handicrafts:

- Beading
- Crocheting
- Knitting (see the next page)
- Lacework (tatting)
- Weaving

Work with sewing:

- Design and/or sew a robe, tabard, cloak, tunic, or stole (see the next page)
- Create other magickal garb: reticules, belts, cingulums, and so forth.

- Create pouches, pillows, bags, book covers, poppets, or scabbards.
- Sew a magickal quilt or banner.

Practice arcane home crafts:

- Work with natural dyes.
- Spin yarn from threads.
- Make soap or natural bath and beauty products.

Work with kitchen magicks:

- Create a kitchen altar.
- Cook with magickal intention.
- Process food or herbs via drying or "canning."

Sample retreat ideas

1. **Learn to knit**. Buy a good book or use the surprisingly excellent YouTube videos available for knitting neophytes. Or, if you already are a knitter, devote your retreat to completing a project start to finish, to tackling a new and difficult project, or to completing a specifically magickal piece of knitting.

2. **Design and create a magickal cloak**. Patterns are available on the Internet and can be purchased in fabric stores, too. Consider a color that matches your magickal intentions, and for best results, purchase a fabric that's practical (i.e., washable) and easy to handle. Cotton is an excellent example, and many people are now working with fleece, especially if they'll be working outdoors in a chilly environment.

3. **Sew dream pillows**. Select herbs (and perhaps some tiny gem chips) associated with dreamwork, relaxation, or astral travel. Select fabrics in colors that support these intentions. Sew small fabric pillows—perhaps six inches square—and stuff them with the herbal mixture. Decorate as desired. Hand-letter instruction cards to go with them; the user should tuck one of the pillows under his or her regular pillow at bedtime for sweet dreams and spectacular adventures.

4. **Create a kitchen altar**. Choose a spot for a kitchen altar; cleanse, bless, and dedicate the space; set up the altar, installing items of your choice (don't forget a kitchen witch, a little witch figurine kept in the kitchen as a talisman of protection and perhaps inspiration); carry out a ritual to open the new altar; and then make a plan to pause there, mindfully, each day.

Sample overnight retreat for sewing a set of robes

Call to adventure:	As my magickal knowledge and skill increase, I'd like to be able to dress the part. I'd like to sew my own robes to wear during ritual and on special magickal occasions.
Type of focus:	Practice, testing, and trial + Seclusion.
Magickal goals:	Finish my robes by the time the retreat ends.
Time:	4:00 p.m. Friday to sometime Saturday evening.
Place:	Amanda's cabin on Mt. Hood. It's on the creek, providing a great place for walking when I need to stretch. I can drive into town nearby if I need wireless access: e.g., to check some sort of sewing instructions on the Web.
Timing details:	Waxing moon-gathering energy. A good time to create.
Magickal activities:	Creation of magickal garb, which I'll be able to use for years to come. I'll also be writing in my magickal journal.
Spiritual activities:	Spellcraft for inspiration and creativity, blessings over food, dedication ritual wearing my new robes.
Mundane activities:	Before the retreat, I'll hit the fabric stores and look through the various robe patterns. I'll need to buy a pattern and the fabric and notions. I'll need to preshrink the fabric before I leave, too. Once at retreat, I'll want to enjoy some time by the creek and in the woods.
Creating mood:	I'm going to bring along my laptop as it has all my music on it. I'm also bringing my "Practical Magick" DVD as I adore it and it puts me in a fun, creative mood.

Embracing silence, slowness, and a quiet pace:	No TV, radio, cell service, or Internet. I can go into town for Internet if I absolutely need it.
Food:	Her cabin has a kitchen, but I'm going to keep it simple. I think I'll plan for sandwiches and take makings for a huge salad. I'll take fruit, too, and instant coffee.
Materials needed:	Pattern, fabric, sewing notions, sewing scissors, sewing machine (I don't hand-sew well enough to make the robes by hand), iron, camera, magickal journal, pens, and a book or two for reading, jar for creek water, baggie for ashes. I'll also want to take outdoor clothes and boots for walking, and probably a rain jacket. And, I'll bring a few things to set up a small altar space for rituals. Oh—and some firewood. Her cabin has a fireplace! I might sleep right out on the couch and enjoy it.
Departure:	As I step into the car, I'll officially enter retreat space. So mote it be!
Schedule:	Friday evening: Arrive before dark. Settle in, start a fire, and have dinner. Set up work area. Perform a brief ritual and/or ask a blessing to the universe that my hands be guided as I work. Turn music on. Lay out fabric and pattern and cut out pieces of future robes. Take photos as I work. Begin a journal page, explaining what I'm doing and adding comments and inspirations. If there's enough fabric, perhaps cut out some pouches or a reticule as well. Late evening: Enjoy the fire; watch "Practical Magick." Sleep. . . Saturday morning: Breakfast, then a walk by the creek and through the woods. Watch for messages from the universe re: my undertakings. Collect a jar of creek water for future magickal works; look for a stone to add to the altar at home. Return to cabin and make a journal entry. Saturday mid-morning: Start sewing! Take photos as the work progresses.

| Schedule continued: | *Noon: Simple lunch. Journal about progress. Read and relax for half an hour or so.*
Afternoon: Keep sewing until robes are complete. Continue with photos and journal entries. Take a mid-afternoon stroll by the creek if needed—or I might prefer to keep working
Late afternoon: Don new robes and carry out a ritual of dedication. If weather permits, do this outdoors and at creekside, perhaps anointing the robes with dabs of creek water and charging them to mother Gaia.
4:00-ish: Pack up. Take some ashes from the fireplace to add to my ashes collection. Offer a blessing for safe travel. Head home, stopping for a snack on the way. |
| Return: | *Greet family. Unpack and show off my new robes. Send Amanda a thank-you card for the loan of her cabin!* |

Notes and Ideas

_____

_____

_____

_____

Suggested Resources for This Chapter

Emery, Carla. *The Encyclopedia of Country Living.* Sasquatch, 2008. (*A compendium of the domestic arts of self-sufficiency.*)

Maresh, Jan Saunders. *Sewing for Dummies, 3rd edition.* Wiley, 2010.

Scarpa, Sandra McCraw. *Magical Fabric Art: Spellwork & Wishcraft through Patchwork Quilting and Sewing.* Llewellyn, 1998.

Telesco, Patricia. *A Kitchen Witch's Cookbook.* Llewellyn, 2002.

Chapter Thirteen

Arts and Crafts Focus

In this type of retreat, arts and crafts take on a magickal angle as you use traditional approaches to adorn and embellish your magickal life. In this group you'll find the traditional arts and handicrafts: everything from working with leather and metalwork to toolcrafting, writing, and fabric arts. Let your creative juices flow . . .

Ideas for a retreat focused on arts and crafts

- Creation and adornment of a wand, stave, athame, or another magickal implement
- Drawing and painting
- Sculpture
- Leather craft
- Metalwork
- Bead craft
- Woodwork and wood burning
- Photography and video
- Fabric arts and crafts: making prayer flags, quilt squares, altar cloths, and more

- Music
- Dance
- Writing crafts
  - Develop or expand a specialized journal.
  - Work with quill and scroll: calligraphy, special pens and papers, or arcane alphabets.
  - Create a magickal tome such as a Book of Shadows or Book of Write.
  - Design a personal sigil.
- Work on creative or personal writing.
- Practice scrapbooking techniques.

Sample retreat ideas

1. **Practice woodcrafting.** Use retreat time to practice or hone your woodworking skills: work with carving, shaping, sanding, waxing, or the like. Practice intricate carving with a handheld rotary tool, using wood "blanks" for your initial practice sessions. Once techniques are mastered, you can use them to shape and adorn magickal tools: wands, staves, panticles, drinking vessels, and so forth. Note that many of these techniques will also work on alternative materials like shells, soft stone (soapstone is excellent for carving), and drinking horns. Don't forget to wear eye protection!

2. **Make and/or adorn a tool.** An entire retreat can easily be devoted to the crafting of magickal tools. In the case of a wand, and depending on the length of your retreat, you might find and prepare the wood (e.g., on a hike or at a fine-woods shop); carve and shape the wand (using hand or power tools, sanding materials); add decorations or adornments (beads, metal wires, gems, crystals, inscriptions, secret cores); finish the wand (paints, sealants, varnish); charge, consecrate, name, and or bless the wand; and even use the wand in ritual.

3. **Work with leather or another unfamiliar medium.** Take the plunge into something you know nothing about. Acquire a number of different pieces of leather and leather-working tools and stamps. Spend the retreat learning to

handle the different materials, and then make a small bag or pouch to serve as a medicine bag or to hold a magickal item.

4. **Make a string of prayer beads.** Research the uses of prayer beads, rosaries, or the like. Contemplate the purpose for your beads—or the ways you'll use them—and design a bead string to fit whatever purpose you have in mind. Select strings, catches, and individual beads according to your purpose. Practice knot tying as well; each knot has its own shape and correspondence, and each can lend magick to your string. Finally, create the string, charge it with energy, and carry out a ritual of first use. All of these steps can be accomplished during your retreat; the step of shopping for the beads and materials might make a fun part of the event, too. Last but not least, you could craft your own beads from a number of materials—e.g., shells, oven-baked polymer clay, or paper.

5. **Craft a set of altar cloths.** Altar cloths are an important part of most altars. They provide an attractive backdrop, catch bits of dripped wax and charred incense, and, through their colors and patterns, help tie together the altar's theme and use. It's always lovely to have a set of cloths to choose from, and you could easily devote a retreat day to their production. Purchase a set of fabrics in desired colors and patterns. Washable, sturdy fabrics are recommended, but something metallic or gauzy is perfect as well. (Note: The period leading up to Samhain is a wonderful time to shop for arcane-patterned fabrics.) Cut the cloths as desired, considering shape: circles, squares, triangles, etc. (One of my magickal friends works with hexagons.) Hem each side, either using a sewing machine or—if you don't sew—iron-on fusible webbing. Adorn as desired, consecrate, and enjoy.

6. **Practice calligraphy and the use of magickal alphabets.** Develop a plan. Do you have a specific use in mind for fine writing, or are you simply interested in practicing calligraphy and/or illumination and learning more about the skills? Gather special papers, pens, and inks, considering colors and textures as you plan. You may want to locate a calligraphy guidebook to help you study and practice lettering and borders. Devote a day or more to working with the different materials. Carry out specific projects as desired or just enjoy working

with the materials themselves. Add a new level of fun by working with different alphabets or scripts: for example, Ogham, Theban, Pictish, or Runic.

7. **Make music.** Develop a retreat devoted to learning or practicing a musical instrument. Include a recording device—or music software on a laptop or iPad—to help you track your progress. Make it a goal to learn at least one piece of music that you could use in ritual or for a magickal gathering. In addition, learn and demonstrate the correct care and tuning (if relevant) of your chosen instrument.

Sample overnight retreat for creating a magickal Book of Write

Call to adventure:	I'm in the midst of a Druid fostership, and I need to create a "Book of Write" to store my Order's litany as well as to track my own progress.
Type of focus:	Practice, testing, and trial
Magickal goals:	I already have a notebook-actually, a three-ring binder-that I want to use, but I want to spend the retreat getting it set up and considering its divisions. I also want to practice lettering, making page borders, and so forth. I'd like to make some of my first entries as part of my sacred retreat. Finally, I plan a ritual of dedication for both the book and myself.
Time:	Friday evening (after work) to Sunday morning
Place:	My home. I plan to make it more retreat-like by leaving my phone off and eschewing TV, Internet for fun, etc. I _will_ enter sacred space.
Timing details:	Full moon on Saturday night.
Magickal activities:	Practice with pens, inks, and lettering. Practice with some of the main points of manuscript illumination. Begin my Book of Write, and dedicate it-and me-to its purpose.
Spiritual activities:	Ritual bath before beginning, hand washing before meals, Saturday evening dedication ritual.

Mundane activities:	Meals, morning and afternoon walks, study periods. I will use the Web to access my Order's materials. (I don't want to waste paper by printing hard copies.)
Creating mood:	Candles, music; will wear robes while working.
Embracing silence, slowness, and a quiet pace:	No TV, radio, cell, or other electronic devices. Will have windows open if weather permits. Soft Celtic music in the background.
Food:	Whatever is at hand—I'll be home. Lots of tea!
Materials needed:	My binder, a collection of special papers, pens of all types and colors, reference books with arcane alphabets, nature journaling book, drawing and sketching book, art materials, eraser, laptop, wide green ribbon (four feet). (Since I'll be home, if I need anything else, it'll be easy to grab it. However, I'm going to try to think ahead and have everything ready.)
Departure:	On Friday evening before bed, I'll set up the dining room table as a work space, and will ask a blessing on my intentions. These actions will signify my entry into retreat space. Saturday morning, I'll wake up, take a ritual bath, and begin.
Schedule:	Friday evening: See "Departure," above. Saturday morning: Wake up, make coffee. Take mug of coffee for a morning walk. Return, take a ritual bath, don robes, and begin. Spend the morning practicing writing, bordering, tiny sketches, symbols (triskele). Saturday noon: Quick lunch. While eating, access Order materials on the Web and decide which aspect of the Litany I'll begin with. Saturday early afternoon: Plan the Book of Write's layout. For example, include a section for the Litany, a section for my progress as a Fosterling, a section for celebration and ritual, one for herb craft, one for full moon work. It's a 3-ring binder, so I can adjust if needed, but having a structure in mind will help the project move forward. Perhaps consider papers and ink colors for each type of entry? And I'll need a title page and a dedication page.

Schedule continued:	*Saturday mid-late afternoon: Begin entering material in my Book of Write. Goal: Create title page, dedication page (which I will sign after the ritual), one or two pages of litany, and a Fosterling/journal entry to commemorate this occasion. Adorn pages with borders and other designs. May decide to place a symbol on upper right page corner-good place for a triskele. Work on more pages if there's time!* *Saturday evening: Dinner, and time to read and relax. Then begin work again. Perhaps spend some time memorizing a piece of litany.* *Later evening: Before bed, carry out a ritual encompassing protection of the Book and my dedication to its purpose. Finish the ritual by signing the dedication page and then tying the green ribbon around it as a gesture of its sanctity and safekeeping. Set the book in a window facing the full moon; leave it to charge overnight. Step outside and spend time with the moon, then head for bed.* *Sunday morning: Retrieve Book from moony window and declare the retreat concluded. Shower, dress, and head out for a celebratory brunch at a favorite local place.*
Return:	*After brunch, clean up everything, then settle in to look through the Book and review yesterday's progress. Make plans to continue.*

Notes and Ideas

_____

_____

_____

_____

Suggested Resources for This Chapter

Greer, John Michael. *Pagan Prayer Beads: Magic and Meditation with Pagan Rosaries.* Weiser, 2007.

Harris, Eleanor and Philip Harris. *The Crafting & Use of Ritual Tools: Step-by-Step Instructions for Woodcrafting Religious & Magical Implements.* Llewellyn, 2002.

Maresh, Jan Saunders. *Sewing for Dummies, 3rd edition.* Wiley, 2010.

MacLir, Alferian Gwydion. *Wandlore: The Art of Crafting the Ultimate Magical Tool.* Llewellyn, 2011.

Pesznecker, Susan. *Crafting Magick with Pen and Ink: Learn to Write Stories, Spells, and Other Magickal Works.* Llewellyn, 2009.

Smedley, Wendy. *Start Scrapbooking: Your Essential Guide to Recording Memories.* Memory Makers, 2010.

Chapter Fourteen

Green Magick Focus

When we practice green magick, we embrace the natural world as a way of life, a teacher, and a focus of undying energy. Then we bring that wisdom inside ourselves, using it as a center for magickal workings whether they're focused on nature, psychic arts, ceremonial magick, or any other type of practice.

Early civilizations practiced nature-based magick as a form of life-affirming spirituality and a way to achieve a sort of communion with Earth, the spirits, and the gods. Natural tools and objects were used as both ritual objects and as a way of focusing energies and conducting magick, and that magick was considered to be a part of everyday life—not something apart from it. Today's green magick continues that practice by using a set of practices and philosophies that have the natural world at their center. In this approach, green magick becomes both form and function, a literal and symbolic representation that guides one's magickal life.

Ideas for a retreat focused on green magick

- Nature studies: Experience and work in one or more outdoor settings
- Naturalist studies: Practice techniques as an amateur naturalist: for example, collecting and pressing plants, making bark rubbings, collecting rocks, plant and tree identification.
- Rockhounding: Work with finding, identifying, and labeling stones

- Herbalism
  - Study a number of herbs.
  - Create your own herbal formulary.
  - Practice herbal techniques, such as preparing decoctions, tinctures, or infusions.
  - Go wildcrafting.
  - Go mushroom or truffle hunting.
- Gardening
  - Design, plant, and/or maintain a garden with specifically magickal intent.
  - Design and plant an herb garden.
  - Design and plant a container garden.
  - Design and establish a water garden.
- Go camping, hiking, or backpacking with the specific intent of engaging with nature.
- Work with nature deities and entities, including the fae.
- Create and dedicate a nature journal.
- Carry out an action that impacts habitat and benefits animals or birds.
- Work with totem animals and spirits.
- Experience and work magick in a sacred natural location.
- Create a magickal construction: e.g., a labyrinth, henge (or stone circle), or medicine circle.

Sample retreat ideas

1. **Hone your naturalist skills.** Acquire a copy of a naturalist guide, and review some of the techniques within. Develop a retreat that allows you to practice them. Establish a rock or shell collection or collect and press a number of tree leaves. Always follow ethical sustainable practices—and get necessary permissions—if collecting.

2. **Work with a nature deity or the fae.** Research the being that you hope to attract or pay homage to, then develop a site in your garden specifically de-

signed to invite that being in for a visit. Consider plantings, colors, elemental allusions, or statuary. Use your retreat time to install and dedicate the garden spot.

3. **Plant a container garden with a specific purpose.** Identify a container for a good-sized container garden; this could be anything from a very large pot to a plastic garbage container (with holes punched) to a hay bale to a raised garden bed. Determine a purpose for the garden: Will you grow medicinal herbs? A kitchen veggie garden? Berries? Develop a plan for locating and setting up the garden. Bless and charge the materials (and seeds) before planting. Devote the retreat to getting the job done, and prepare to enjoy the rewards in weeks to come.

4. **Take a hike!** Set one or more goals in advance: You might be looking for day signs or augurs, searching for wood for a wand or stave, aiming to identify as many birds as possible, or looking for sacred space. Bring along camera, journal, field guides, and any other necessary materials. Don't forget to take along the Ten Outdoor Essentials (chapter 5), snacks, and water, and file a detailed trip plan so someone knows where you are.

5. **Create a henge.** A henge is a monument consisting of upright stones or pieces of wood, usually arranged in a circle. Use stones or pieces of wood to create a henge in one corner of your yard. Adjust the size accordingly, but work in "threes" if possible—i.e., keeping the dimensions divisible by three (for magickal impact). You may wish to research sacred geometric techniques, allowing you to measure and construct the henge with only a rope and peg. Consider placing an altar or something similar in the henge's center. Finish the work by conducting a ritual within the bounds.

Sample one-day retreat for a wildcrafting outing

Call to adventure:	*I'm getting pretty comfortable with my herbal knowledge and preparations, but I need to learn more about herbs in their natural habitats.*
Type of focus:	*Practice, testing, and trial*

Magickal goals:	Carry out a wildcrafting outing in a location where it's acceptable to gather herbs. I'll identify and gather several and will prepare them for storage. I'll study them as well.
Time:	Wednesday morning and afternoon
Place:	Mt. Hood National Forest—one hour southeast; also my home.
Timing details:	Sunny skies needed. If it rains or snows, I'll reschedule for the next week.
Magickal activities:	Gathering and preparation of herbs, awareness of natural world and green magick; awareness of sacred spaces.
Spiritual activities:	Safe travel ritual; also, a general mindfulness/attentiveness in the outdoors.
Mundane activities:	Hike and plant collection, picnic lunch. Call the Mt. Hood National Forest office the week before and verify whether a permit is needed for gathering. Review identification of poison oak and nettles.
Creating mood:	Being outdoors! (Nothing else needed!)
Embracing silence, slowness, and a quiet pace:	Again: being outdoors. Will carry cell phone—turned off—for emergencies.
Food:	Picnic lunch, GORP, and a couple of quarts of water.
Materials needed:	Sunhat and sunglasses; plant shears (my trusty Felco #75); field guide of western herbs; camera, backpack; newspaper; large Ziploc bags; journal and pens; index cards and indelible marker; gathering permit (if needed); Ten Outdoor Essentials (chapter 5); cell phone.
Departure:	As I begin hiking, I will pause and be mindfully aware of my entry into the sacred outdoors.
Schedule:	Morning: Have breakfast then drive to Mt. Hood. Park car in a public area, if possible. Enter the woods—stay on trail. Find a spot to settle and carry out a quiet half-hour observation, working to polish and activate observation skills. Journal about the results.

Schedule continued:	*Throughout the day:* Continue hiking, watching for herbal stands. Clarify identification with field guides. Go at least 50-75 feet off-trail before gathering. Follow ethical wildcrafting guidelines. Photograph each stand/herb before cutting. Wrap cut herbs in newspaper and then place in plastic bags; include index card with name of plant, time found, and location found. Eat when hungry. Remember to drink water! *Afternoon:* Return to car and head home. Once home, unbundle plants. Soak in a basin of salt water to release dirt and organisms. Rinse, pat dry gently, and arrange to dry on absorbent paper-lined cookie sheets. Take more photos. Begin research on each herb and make journal entries.
Return:	Unpack and put everything away. Wash plant shears and wipe blades lightly with veggie oil. Place trays of herbs in a warm room out of direct sunlight. Plan to "stir" daily until dry.

Notes and Ideas

Suggested Resources for This Chapter

Andrews, Ted. *Animal Speak: The Spiritual and Magickal Powers of Creatures Great and Small.* Llewellyn, 1996.

Artress, Lauren. *Walking a Sacred Path: Rediscovering the Labyrinth as a Spiritual Practice.* Riverhead Trade, 2006.

Baker, Nick. *The Amateur Naturalist.* National Geographic, 2005.

Cunningham, Scott. *Earth Power: Techniques of Natural Magic.* Llewellyn, 2002.

Drew, A. J. *A Wiccan Formulary and Herbal.* New Page Books, 2004.

Dugan, Ellen. *Garden Witch's Herbal: Green Magick, Herbalism & Spirituality.* Llewellyn, 2009.

Leslie, Clare Walker, and Charles E. Roth. *Keeping a Nature Journal: Discover a Whole New Way of Seeing the World Around You.* Storey, 2003.

Moura, Ann. *Green Witchcraft III: The Manual.* Llewellyn, 2000.

Pellant, Chris. *Rocks and Minerals (Smithsonian Handbook).* DK Adult, 2002.

Peterson Field Guides. Houghton Mifflin Harcourt, various years. (*These pocket guides are available for every type of natural observation—birds, trees, weather, herbs, etc.— and for many specific geological areas, too.*)

Chapter Fifteen

Physical and Magickal Wellness Focus

What better way to practice magick than to work with one's own body, increasing its strength and vigor? The better your overall health, the stronger your body; and the more vital your energy, the more actively you'll be able to embrace the magickal realm and, presumably, the better your magick.

Ideas for a retreat focused on personal wellness and challenge

- Develop and carry out a physical challenge: a long walk, ride, run, hike, swim, remote campout, or something else. This might be a one-time "big event" or the initiation of a new exercise plan.

- Elemental challenge: Select a significant challenge that references one or more of the cardinal elements: e.g., rock climbing or caving (earth); scuba diving or snorkeling (water); fire walking or a desert visit (fire); skydiving, a high-ropes course, or a zip line (air).

- Study and practice a healing discipline, such as medicinal herbalism, reflexology, Reiki, pranic healing, or chromatherapy.

- Engage in healing work for yourself or someone else.

- Pamper yourself with a self-styled spa weekend.
- Practice a martial art or a discipline such as tai chi or yoga.
- Conduct a detailed health survey; plan and initiate a personal health overhaul.

Sample retreat ideas

1. **Take a five-mile walk.** Plan a five-mile walk that will provide interesting sites and perhaps some physical challenge. Dress in layers and wear good walking shoes. Carry snacks, water, and a cell phone, as well as personal ID. Read this charm as you begin: *Strong my heart, and fleet my feet, soon to start, my blood to beat. Send me power that I may last for hours and hours along this path.* As you walk, be aware of the world around you, of your blood pumping, your heart beating, the wind moving, birds singing. Feel your immersion into natural space. Watch for day signs and augurs. Once home, journal about the experience and reflect on its impact.

2. **Study reflexology.** Use resource materials to learn about reflexology. Practice some of the techniques on yourself, and consider the results. Try copying sketches of hand, foot, and ear reflexology points into your journal. Make a plan to continue working with the practices and perhaps to try them on friends or family members.

3. **Practice tai chi.** If you know tai chi, use a retreat to practice what you know, to carry out longer or repeated practice sessions, or to learn new movements and patterns. If you do not know tai chi, obtain an introductory DVD and use your retreat experience to practice the initial movements and routines. In addition, use written materials to study tai chi and its background. Journal about your experiences, developing a plan that will motivate you to keep exploring.

Sample overnight retreat for a spa weekend

Call to adventure:	*I'm pooped! I've been working too hard and taking care of everyone but myself. I need to get away! It's time to devote some time to ME.*
Type of focus:	*Seclusion + Sanctuary + Escape!*

Magickal goals:	Carry out a "rejampering" (rejuvenation + pampering) retreat, devoted solely to me.
Time:	2 p.m. Monday to dinner time (approx.) on Tuesday
Place:	Fancy hotel downtown on the river! (This is all about luxury, and I've been saving my money!) The room includes a soaker tube, plasma TV, WiFi, balcony view, fridge, and microwave (plus coffee/coffeemaker, an herbal tea assortment, bottled water, and microwave popcorn). The hotel includes a restaurant, pool, gym, and spa/salon.
Timing details:	Monday is the Moon's day, and an ideal time for feminine-type nurturing. The dark moon is two days earlier, so although the moon will be in a waxing phase, the energy will still be somewhat subdued.
Magickal activities:	Work with Tarot; use of herbs, stones, and essential oils as part of the spa experience. Focus on self as a vital magickal being!
Spiritual activities:	Work in a ritual for self-empowerment.
Mundane activities:	None of this retreat will be mundane! But seriously, I plan to sleep, bathe, swim, exercise, get massaged, and just have a great time. I'll make all spa and salon appointments in advance.
Creating mood:	LED candles and a gas fireplace in hotel room; 42-inch plasma screen for R&R; peace and quiet!
Embracing silence, slowness, and a quiet pace:	Simply being on my own time will help with this. I may or may not use WiFi or watch TV. My goal is to do whatever I need to do to emerge feeling pampered and with energy restored.
Food:	All at the hotel! Room service dinner in my room. Microwave popcorn in the evening. Brunch in the dining room on Tuesday.
Materials needed:	Clothing, personal items, swimsuit, exercise wear, journal, pens, camera, laptop & cord, Tarot cards, a book or two.
Departure:	As I walk into the hotel, I'll pause briefly and declare my retreat to have begun!

Schedule:	*Approximate schedule* (All subject to change, except for spa appointments!) Monday, 2 p.m.: Check into hotel. Settle into room. Do a Tarot spread to gauge the course of my retreat. Leave cards in place for later review. (Take a photo of them, too.) Change into bathing suit and go for a swim. Use the immersion as a sense of intentionally immersing in the retreat experience. Finish with some time in the hot tub. 4 p.m.: Return to room. Enjoy bottled water, peaceful music (laptop). Contemplate Tarot cards a bit more. Dress in exercise clothing and go to spa at 4:30 for hot stone massage. Mmmmm . . . 5:30: Return to room. Make a cup of herbal tea and journal about experiences so far. Review Tarot spread and work on interpretation. 6:15: Go for a walk on and around the hotel grounds. Buy a postcard in the gift shop. Pick up a candy bar for later. 7:00-ish: Order room service dinner! Pull out all stops! When dinner arrives, offer a blessing over the food, then enjoy the meal, maybe watching TV or reading. After dinner: Anything is possible! Watch a movie with popcorn. Read, work with Tarot cards, or journal. Maybe go hot-tubbing or swimming again. Perhaps order a room service dessert. Whatever! Revel in the luxury. Warm bath before bed . . . Tuesday morning: Up early: Shower, dress, and go to the dining room for brunch. 9:00: Spa appointment for mud wrap and massage. Mmmm . . .Swim afterward. Return to room and create a second Tarot spread to consider my directions after the retreat ends. Journal . . . Tuesday mid-day: Pack up. Carry out a quick ritual of self-empowerment to capture the restorative energy. Check out of hotel, leaving bags at front desk. Go to salon for mani-pedi, facial, and hair styling.
Return:	Leave hotel. Return home, feeling unaccountably spoiled and luxuriant. Greet family. Start saving money for next time!

Notes and Ideas

_____

_____

_____

_____

Suggested Resources for This Chapter

Bardey, Catherine. *Secrets of the Spas: Pamper and Vitalize Yourself at Home.* Black Dog & Leventhal, 1999.

Bennett, Robin Rose. *Healing Magic: A Green Witch Guidebook.* Sterling, 2004.

Drew, A. J. *A Wiccan Formulary and Herbal.* New Page Books, 2004.

Sullivan, Tammy. *Elemental Witch: Fire, Air, Water, Earth; Discover Your Natural Affinity.* Llewellyn, 2006.

Chapter Sixteen

Psychic Arts Focus

Psychic arts are "mind magicks." In this type of retreat, you'll work to develop and hone the powers of your mind and intuition. Divination is also a type of psychic art, and you might choose a retreat allowing you to study or learn more about a specific divinatory practice.

Ideas for a retreat focused on psychic arts

- Work with specific mind magicks: e.g., memory, telepathy, clairvoyance, psychokinesis, or aura work.
- Dream work (only for an overnight stay, of course)
- Astral voyaging
- Basic energy practices: grounding, centering, shielding, aura work
- Chakra work
- Ascetic practices: fasting, meditation, silence
- Divination work:
  - Tarot (See also chapter 3)
  - Pendulum
  - Ogham

- Runes
- Tasseomancy (tea-leaf reading)
- Scrying
- Other divining tools or oracles

- Create your own oracle.
- Work with augury—the "seeing" and reading of omens or augurs.

Sample retreat ideas

1. **Have a mind magicks-athon.** Devote a retreat period to practicing one or more mental arts: for example, telepathy, clairvoyance, or psychokinesis. You might work with a playing card deck of Zener cards. Journal before and after in order to assess your progress.

2. **Work on core energy practices.** Polish your core energy practices with focused work on grounding, centering, shielding, and work with your aura. These practices are, after all, the heart of all energy work. Put them to work: ground and center before meditation or ritual, or perhaps visit a public place, shield, and see how effectively you can fall into the background. Learn to project or dim your aura as a basic aspect of magick protection.

3. **Make and work with a scrying mirror.** Use a picture frame with a glass insert (not Plexiglas) and glossy black paint. Remove the glass, paint the background and the frame black, allow to dry, and reassemble. Voilà—an inexpensive scrying tool. Charge it under the dark moon and wrap in black cloth when not in use. Devote a retreat to making, dedicating, and working with the mirror. You can try scrying with other materials as well: for example, a crystal ball, fire, candle flame, or silver bowl filled with water. Journal about your results.

4. **Create your own oracle.** Develop a plan for making your own oracle. Consider in advance the information you will hope to receive, and design elements that will respond in those ways. Consider whether you'll develop "suits"—akin to the Tarot—or simply a single set of related components. You could use cards (as with the Tarot), discs (as with runes), stones, or something else. Consider the importance of numbers, symbols, and images in designing your oracle.

Complete the pieces, consecrate in some way, and begin using them. Prepare to make adjustments before eventually arriving at an end point. Careful journaling will help you judge how well the oracle is working.

5. **Practice augury.** Where divination uses a tool in order to understand or "divine" meaning, augury requires the use of one's observational powers and awareness to see and interpret naturally occurring signs. You might spend a day looking for a particular type of natural augur: for example, cloud patterns, arrangements of twigs or pebbles, birds in flight. Record what you see, hear, and sense, and be aware of what you think they might indicate. Journal your findings and interpretations, and compare them to resource materials about natural augury.

Sample overnight retreat for work with creating and empowering runes

Call to adventure:	I'd like to learn more about runes and would like to start by making a set of my own. I'd also like to create a unique bindrune or perhaps a runic sigil of my own.
Type of focus:	Practice, testing, and trial + Vigil + Vision Quest
Magickal goals:	Create and dedicate a set of polymer clay runes. Create a bindrune or sigil.
Time:	Tuesday morning to Wednesday morning; full moon Wednesday around 2:00 a.m.
Place:	My home. I live alone, and I can make use of home materials and my oven in carrying out the retreat. I will also use my outdoor fire pit for vigil.
Timing details:	Wednesday is an excellent time for inspiration and divination—a good time for a vigil experience.
Magickal activities:	Create the runes.
Spiritual activities:	Dedicate the runes. Conduct an overnight vigil "sitting by" them; meditate on a bindrune or sigil. Include a ritual of thanks/completion.
Mundane activities:	Meals, fire building

Creating mood:	Gregorian chant music. (It always feels kind of arcane to me.)
Embracing silence, slowness, and a quiet pace:	Home alone, no TV, no Internet, no phone.
Food:	Whatever is on hand. Will go out for breakfast on Wednesday morning after the retreat ends.
Materials needed:	Polymer clay (beige, to look "stony"), food scale, sharp kitchen knives, chips of clear quartz, permanent black markers, quick-dry matte sealer for polymer clay, small brushes, small drawstring bag (could make this during the retreat if I decide to), books about runes, warm cloak, firewood (lots!) and matches, flashlight, paper and pencil, journal, camera, camp chair, fantasy novel for reading (Raymond Feist, maybe), cloak, magick pendant, clean altar cloth.
Departure:	The work begins when I get out of bed. So mote it be.
Schedule:	Tuesday morning: up (no alarm), shower, dress, simple oatmeal breakfast. Pause for a moment of intention, asking guidance on my activities. Tuesday mid-morning: Use my rune resources to practice writing each runic character. Shape and cut the polymer clay into thick square discs—I'm going for squares, rather than circles, because I want to reference the cardinal elements. Use a food scale to weigh each blob of clay and ensure even size. Push a tiny quartz chip (for divinatory powers and insights) into each one, smoothing over the insertion mark. Use marker to inscribe the runic symbol on each one, leaving the opposite side blank. Work carefully, making the tiles as smooth and identical as possible. Include two tiles that are blank on both sides. Take photographs as I work. Bake and cool as directed. Lunch: Whenever—depends on how the process goes.

Schedule continued:	Afternoon: Brush completed runes with quick-drying polymer sealer; allow first side to dry then do the second side. While they dry, begin work on a bindrune and/or sigil. Draw several possibilities, considering the qualities desired and the design itself. Journal about the day's work so far, including the details.
	Dinner: Make dinner. Read and relax. Perhaps take a brief nap in preparation for vigil.
	Evening: Set up a journal page for each separate rune. Select one and begin reading/researching about it, adding details and diagrams to the magick journal. Practice writing words using the runic alphabet to become more familiar with their meanings and use.
	Late evening: After the runes are dry (should take about 2 hours per side), carry out "draws" and a simple reading, following instructions in resource guides. Journal about the results, and photograph the first spread.
	11:30 p.m.: Clean up my work. Place the cooled runes into their drawstring bag. Don cloak and magickal jewelry, and have runes, flashlight, and bindrune/sigil drawings at hand, as well as my journal, pens, altar cloth, and camera. Go to the campfire pit. At midnight, lay and light a fire. Carry out a ritual of opening and create sacred space. Spread the runes over the altar cloth, allowing them to charge in the moon and firelight.
	Sit vigil with the runes, meditating on the potential bindrunes and sigils until a message is received re: which are "real" and "true." If possible, sit vigil through the night, meditating and holding each rune in turn. In addition, search for a new name as a rune crafter. Take photographs as appropriate.
	Wednesday morning: Great the sunrise. If I took a new or additional name, I'll speak it aloud to the rising sun: "I am _____." I'll gather the runes, close the sacred circle, make sure the fire is out, and return to the house. I'll declare the retreat ended.
Return:	Head out for celebratory breakfast. Journal about the experience upon return. Keep the runes close/ on my person for the next 7 days for magickal bonding.

Notes and Ideas

Suggested Resources for This Chapter

Allrich, Karri. *A Witch's Book of Dreams: Understanding the Power of Dreams & Symbols.* Llewellyn, 2001.

Carlin, Emily. *Defense Against the Dark: A Field Guide to Protecting Yourself from Predatory Spirits, Energy Vampires, and Malevolent Magick.* New Page Books, 2011. (*This wonderful book does triple duty. First, it's a Field Guide for the Dark Arts and Creatures of the Night. Second, it's a manual of core energy practices. And third, it's a compendium of protective magicks.*)

Cuhulain, Kerr. *Magickal Self Defense: A Quantum Approach to Warding.* Llewellyn, 2008. (*An excellent book for learning core energy work and practices.*)

Ellison, Rev. Robert Lee "Skip." *Ogham: The Secret Language of the Druids.* ADF Publishing, 2008.

Judith, Anodea. *Chakra Balancing.* Sounds True, 2006.

Moore, Barbara. *Tarot for Beginners: A Practical Guide to Reading the Cards.* Llewellyn, 2010.

Paxson, Diana L. *Taking Up the Runes: A Complete Guide to Using Runes in Spells, Rituals, Divination, and Magic.* Weiser, 2005.

Chapter Seventeen

Cosmological Practices Focus

Magickal folks have always watched and learned from the skies, and your retreat—weather permitting—may provide you with an excellent chance for sky watching. You might want to spend the night outside, sleeping under the stars, or you might simply lie out on a blanket for an hour or two, watching the heavens roll by overhead. Cosmological study seeks to explore and understand the heavens. Whether you practice astrology, astronomy, or celestial magicks, you'll touch the power of the multiverse.

Ideas for a retreat focused on cosmological magicks

- Astrology
- Practice techniques of naked-eye astronomy:
  - Tracking celestial movements
  - Measuring distance and direction in the celestial sphere
  - Identifying heavenly bodies
- Practice techniques of optic-assisted astronomy:
  - Use of binoculars
  - Use of telescope

- Practice celestial magicks:
  - Practice spellwork involving celestial influences.
  - Work with a heavenly deity or patron.
  - Work with a celestial specialty, such as a meteor shower, eclipse, or the northern lights.
  - Craft celestial potions, balms, or talismans.
- Study the moon, moon phases, and zodiacal procession.
- Study the planetary hours or the signs of the zodiac.
- Study a planet, heavenly body, or constellation.
- Work with or make a tool for astronomy:
  - Planisphere
  - Sundial (see the next page)
  - Astrolabe
  - Orrery
  - Astronomy software or applications, such as that available for a laptop, iPad, or smartphone.

Sample retreat ideas

1. **Astrology.** Devote a retreat to studying some aspect of astrology. For example, you could learn to read a birth chart, obtain and decipher your own birth chart, study zodiacal movements, or compare different astrological traditions.

2. **Craft a set of celestial talismans.** Research the deities associated with the visible heavenly bodies, and study their related correspondences. For each deity, inscribe a wood "cookie" or a round wooden or cardboard disc with relevant words, numbers, and symbols. Make detailed journal entries describing the nature and content of each talisman. Charge them under the night sky, making a careful journal entry of which heavenly bodies are overhead. Tuck the talismans away and save them for specific work or until they are needed.

3. **Work magick under the full moon.** Hold your retreat on a full moon evening and preferably on a Monday night. Before the retreat, use moon-charged wa-

ters to create an infusion of lemon and violet (associated with lunar energies), and spend time studying the moon's magickal correspondences as well as one or two associated deities. Work ritual under the moonlight. Pour the infused mixture into a silver bowl, meditating on the moon as you either raise energy to the moon or draw down the moon's energy during your ritual. Use the silver bowl as a scrying focus to divine inspiration, then anoint your magickal tools with the mixture, empowering them to the moon's use. Close the ritual, sitting out under the moon for long enough to follow her movements through the night sky. As you sit vigil, journal about the ritual and sketch the moon's path and appearance. Pour the infused waters back into the earth, giving thanks.

4. **Make a working sundial.** The Web has many models for paper sundials. Download one or more, make them, and practice using them. Read and study more about the process, and about how people used sundials to keep time. Use what you've learned to plan and/or establish a working sundial in your yard or garden (depending on the length of your retreat). Use one of your sundials to time rituals or other magickal activities.

5. **Work with a piece of astronomy software.** The ancient magicians, Witches, and Druids studied and learned the movements of the heavens and used them to time and track their seasonal magickal practices. Hold a nighttime retreat and practice using astronomy modeling software, such as "Starry Night" (PC and Mac) or "Star Walk" (iPad). Work with it until you can use it smoothly to find your way around the night sky. Journal about your actions and results. Make a plan to use your new skills to assist with timing some sort of magick or ritual.

Sample one-night retreat for work with naked-eye astronomy

Call to adventure:	I'd like to be able to look up at night and know what I'm seeing. I'd like to understand how the night sky moves, just like the ancient wizards and alchemists used to.
Type of focus:	Practice, testing, and trial

Magickal goals:	Learn more about the night sky, including identifying and tracking specific constellations and planets.
Time:	Saturday night, into the wee hours
Place:	Rooster Rock State Park (RRSP), which is out of the city and away from lights.
Timing details:	Clear skies needed. If the skies are cloudy, I'll reschedule.
Magickal activities:	Make charged waters for various magickal crafts.
Spiritual activities:	Conduct a short ritual in which I draw down energy from or acknowledge my relationship to the heavens.
Mundane activities:	Practice basic sky-watching skills, such as identifying constellations, spotting planets, measuring distance and elevation using my hands and fingers, and understanding the pattern of celestial movements. I'll also work with a planisphere.
Creating mood:	No need—I'll have the night sky overhead. NOTE: I may take another person along for safety purposes. If I do, he'll be in tune with my goals and will be a working part of the retreat.
Embracing silence, slowness, and a quiet pace:	Easy! I'll be outdoors at night.
Food:	Thermos of cocoa, a couple of sandwiches.
Materials needed:	Flashlight with bulb end covered with red cellophane (or use a red LED light), journal, pens and pencils, jar of spring water, planisphere (buy one or make one), a sky guide (book), warm clothes, wool blanket, comfortable recliner chair, compass.
Departure:	As I step into the car to drive to Rooster Rock, the retreat will begin.

Schedule:	Approximate schedule: Before leaving, look at a current star chart and identify one or two heavily objects visible in the current night sky. Study them long enough to commit them to memory; in addition, do some research on their magickal attributes, etc. Take an evening nap and have a good dinner before beginning.
Schedule continued:	Arrive at RRSP well after dark. Set up viewing area and take time for eyes to acclimate. Begin working through each of the proposed activities, stopping to journal from time to time. Use red lighting to maintain dark adaptation. Locate the objects studied pre-retreat and sketch their positions; at half-hour periods, re-examine the night sky and notice how the heavenly positions have changed, sketching the changes. Use a compass to verify directions. Continue working and watching the night sky for at least 3-4 hours, tracking changes and noting new observations: e.g., the ability to detect star colors, satellites, and the like. Notice whether a specific star, constellation, or other heavenly body seems to attract me. Consider this a heavenly message of some sort, or a natural augur. Conduct a brief ritual under the night sky, asking for inspiration, or perhaps showing my awareness as part of the always-changing multiverse. Head home; if not too tired, journal about the evening experiences. Sleep! In the morning, return to the journal and continue collecting details of the experience. Focus in particular on (a) skills developed and (b) items of special interest. Plan deeper investigation of the latter, and consider how they might inform/enliven my magickal practice.
Return:	Greet family. Put materials away. Journal about the experience.

Notes and Ideas

Suggested Resources for This Chapter

Conway, D. J. *Moon Magick: Myth & Magic, Crafts & Recipes, Rituals & Spells.* Llewellyn, 2002.

Dinwiddie, Robert, et al. *Universe.* DK Adult, 2008.

George, Demetra and Douglas Birch. *Astrology for Yourself: How to Understand and Interpret Your Own Birth Chart.* Ibis, 2006. (*An excellent introductory text for those new to astrology, but detailed enough for the experienced user as well.*)

Henes, Donna. *Celestially Auspicious Occasions: Seasons, Cycles, & Celebrations.* Perigee, 1996.

Lippincott, Kristen. *Astronomy (DK Eyewitness Books).* DK Children, 2008. (*An image-rich guide that provides a wonderful introduction to astronomy.*)

We'Moon: Gaia Rhythms for Womyn. Mother Tongue Ink, 2011. (*Published continually since 1980, this annual combines a datebook format with art, poetry, readings, moon lore, and astrology. Although decidedly woman-centered, it is full of wonderful magick and interpersonal insights that anyone could use.*)

Zell-Ravenheart, Oberon. *Companion for the Apprentice Wizard.* New Page Books, 2004. (*A detail-packed sequel to Zell-Ravenheart's* Grimoire.)

———. *Grimoire for the Apprentice Wizard.* New Page Books, 2004. (*This book, which has been described as a "Boy Scout Handbook for magick users," is rich with "how-tos" and tables of correspondences, planetary hours, rituals, spellwork, and the like.*)

Chapter Eighteen

Ceremonial or Ritual Magick Focus

If you love to do ritual or are fascinated with ceremonial magicks, this retreat may be perfect for you. You might focus on an already established practice, work with something brand new, develop fresh rituals, or even research an area of interest.

Ideas for a retreat focused on ceremony or ritual

- Work with the basic components of ritual craft in your tradition, practicing until you can carry out a ritual order seamlessly (and enjoyably).

- Study or practice one or more ceremonial magick practices, such as practicing the banishing rituals of the pentagram or working with the hierarchies of angels and demons.

- Celebrate a holy day of your choice (e.g., Earth Day).

- Develop (and perhaps carry out) a ritual or rite:

  - A dedication ritual

  - A ritual for completion or rite of passage

  - A naming ritual

  - A ritual to honor a specific event: e.g., a Sabbat, Esbat, or holy day

  - A ritual to consecrate tools for ceremonial magick

• Study and work with a particular deity or patron.

• Study a magickal discipline related to ritual practice: e.g., Hermeticism, the Rosicrucians, or Enochian magick.

• Study and work with a magickal culture or tradition, such as the Mayans or the Egyptians.

• Study the Qabalah (Kabbalah)

Sample retreat ideas

1. **Practice basic ritual craft as per your tradition.** Select a specific element or elements of ritual according to your own practices. For example, you could practice casting a circle, calling the watchtowers, setting and lighting a ritual fire, smudging, "orating," or perfecting songs or chants.

2. **Practice and perfect the Lesser Banishing Ritual of the Pentagram.** Practice the LBRP and possibly other elements of ceremonial ritual, aiming to perfect your movements and voice. Journal about your procedures and results. Develop a plan for practice and implementation. Perhaps use your new techniques for an in-retreat ritual. Or, you might develop teaching materials for sharing your new ideas with others in your magickal group.

3. **Develop a ritual for use on a specific Sabbat.** Select an upcoming Sabbat, confirming the time and day. Develop practices, crafts, magick, or ritual that would be appropriate for your own tradition. You could use the early part of your retreat for the research and planning, concluding with the actual activities themselves (to which others might be invited). Use the opportunity to begin a dedicated section in your magickal journal for each of the eight Sabbats.

4. **Research and study the practice of Hermeticism.** Read materials, study them, and reflect on their meaning in your own magickal tradition. Prepare study aids, and transcribe some of the sacred writings into your own magickal journal. Perhaps outline a course of study.

Sample overnight retreat honoring completion of a magickal passage

Call to adventure:	I am completing my year-and-a-day study of Wicca. I want to do something special to mark this occasion. I also still haven't settled on a craft name.
Type of focus:	Vigil + Vision Quest (Rite of Passage)
Magickal goals:	Spend time reviewing and/or undergoing testing of what I've learned. Then, "garb up" and carry out a formal overnight vigil to honor my passage to the next step. Also, I'll meditate on and find a new craft name.
Time:	Thursday afternoon to Friday morning.
Place:	My home.
Timing details:	The calendar end of my year-and-a-day training.
Magickal activities:	Review of my basic skills that afternoon: My HPS mentor is going to come by and administer a formal test. Assuming I pass, she'll present me with my Level 1 cingulum and I'll move into my retreat.
Spiritual activities:	Ritual bath and donning of magickal garb and jewelry, followed by a deeply ritualized overnight vigil and rite of passage.
Mundane activities:	None.
Creating mood:	Fire: Either outdoors (fire pit), if weather permits, or indoors (fireplace) if it's raining.
Embracing silence, slowness, and a quiet pace:	Silence without and within. Once I pass the testing, I will not speak until the vigil is complete.
Food:	None. Water only. From the time of testing, I will fast until the ritual is complete.
Materials needed:	Frankincense soap; magickal journal and pens; craft robes and cloak, jewelry, and apprentice cingulum (white); Level 1 cingulum (royal blue); wand; firewood and matches; flashlight; comfortable chair (either indoors or out); bottled water; magickal tools and journal/Book of Shadows; compass.

Departure:	The beginning of my ritual will be indicated by my passing the tests. My HPS mentor will inform of this and will lay silence upon me at that moment.
Schedule:	*Thursday during the day:* Review all study materials and practices, preparing for test. I'll have a meal in the mid-afternoon, preparing for the long fast.
	4:00 p.m.: HPS mentor arrives to administer the test. If I pass, she will lay down the silence and hand me my Level 1 cingulum. I will maintain silence, and from that point, my retreat will begin. Note: Turn phones off at this point and set up vigil area (arrange chair, lay fire, etc.).
	5:00-ish: Ritual bath; frankincense soap, clean towels, and other preparations. Don robes and apprentice cingulum. Spend the evening in study and journaling.
	One hour after dark: Process to vigil site, carrying all magickal tools and Book of Shadows, plus the Level 1 cingulum. Conduct a silent ritual, create sacred space, and light fire.
	Sit vigil through the night, watching over the tools and contemplating the new path. Maintain silence. Journal as insights come. Meditate on a craft name and open awareness to messages, inspirations, and perhaps the arrival of various guardians. (One never knows!)
	As dawn arrives, allow the fire to burn down. Stand, remove white cingulum, and replace it with the blue one. Proclaim new craft name to the four directions, ending with east, the direction of the rising sun. Release the circle/sacred space, and declare the ritual ended. Return to house (with magickal tools and journal). Have some orange juice to break the fast.
	Change into street clothes and drive to coven gathering at a local breakfast spot. Greet them with my new craft name; they will give a ritual reply, and at that point, the rite of passage ends, and I will be a newly anointed Level 1 member of the coven, ready for the next level of mysteries to present themselves.

Return:	*Arrive home after breakfast. Carefully stow magickal regalia and equipment. Arrange the new blue cingulum in a place of honor on my altar space. Settle in for detailed journal entries that summarize my experience, and for a formal entry in my BoS. Then, take a nap!*

Notes and Ideas

_____

_____

_____

_____

Suggested Resources for This Chapter

Alexander, Jane. *Sacred Rituals at Home.* Sterling, 2000.

Conway, D. J. *Moon Magick: Myth & Magic, Crafts & Recipes, Rituals & Spells.* Llewellyn, 2002.

Cuhulain, Kerr. *Modern Knighthood: Unleashing Your Inner Warrior to Master Yourself and Your World.* Smashwords (e-book), 2010.

Hall, Manly K. *The Secret Teachings of All Ages.* Wilder, 2009. (*A gorgeous book, filled with the arcane knowledge of the ages and illustrated with striking full-color plates.*)

Jordan, Michael. *Ceremonies for Life.* Collins and Brown, 2001.

K, Amber. *Ritual Craft: Creating Rites for Transformation and Celebration.* Llewellyn, 2006.

Llewellyn's Sabbats Almanac. Llewellyn, published annually.

Regardie, Israel, and Pat Zalewski. *Ceremonial Magic: A Guide to the Mechanisms of Ritual.* Aeon, 2008.

We'Moon: Gaia Rhythms for Womyn. Mother Tongue Ink, 2011. (*Published continually since 1980, this annual combines a datebook format with art, poetry, readings, moon lore, and astrology. Although decidedly woman-centered, it is full of wonderful magick and interpersonal insights that anyone could use.*)

Zell-Ravenheart, Oberon, and Morning Glory Zell-Ravenheart. *Creating Circles and Ceremonies: Rituals for All Seasons and Reasons.* New Page Books, 2006.

Dark Arts Focus

Are you curious about the nether worlds? Would you like to learn or practice protective magicks? Are you interested in studying some of the legend and lore of dark arts and the creatures of the night? A dark arts focus might prove fascinating.

Ideas for a retreat focused on dark arts

- Practice precautionary or protective magicks: shields, wards, banishings, cleansings, projecting an aura of invisibility, and the like.

- Study and practice defensive magicks, such as repulsing shields, severings, bindings, and counter-hexes.

- Craft an amulet or talisman specifically for protection.

- Research, create, and install some form of protective magick around your own home or property.

- Study the use of specific symbols associated with protection or hex magick: e.g., the Evil Eye, Pennsylvania Dutch hex symbols, or specific runes and bindrunes.

- Explore other kids of protective magicks, such as empowering guardians, servitors, poppets, or egregores.

- Explore or study demons, vampires, or other traditional creatures of the night.

- Study the dark arts in more depth, perhaps learning more about psychic attacks, magickal pests, malevolent entities, or other "paranormal activities."
- Study the nature and history of malevolent magicks, such as curses, hexes, and malicious spells.
- Explore the "warrior" mythos and its role in protective magicks.

Sample retreat ideas

1. **Practice basic protective magicks.** Begin with a review of basic energy practices: grounding, centering, moving energy, forming shields. Move into complex shields and then into cleansings and warding. Place protective wards around your home or some other dwelling, and develop a plan for periodically reinforcing them. Journal about your process and results.

2. **Create witch bottles**. Research the idea of protective magicks around one's home and bounds, focusing on the tradition of witch bottles. Prepare a number of witch bottles, charging and empowering each one in ritual. Bury them in appropriate places on your property; you might share one or two with magickal friends. You could even create a mini-bottle to tuck into the glove box of your car.

3. **Study and explore the creatures of the night.** Pick one or more, gather your materials, and delve into a detailed exploration. Ask yourself which commonly held beliefs are true and which are not—you may be surprised. Journal about your discoveries, including the specifics of how to discourage or get rid of unwanted critters if they drop by.

4. **Study the dark arts in more depth.** Satisfy your curiosity by devoting a day or two of study to an often misunderstood magickal subject: the dark arts. Sink into a book on the subject, absorbing and taking notes on the ideas. Your work may suggest projects to complete or additional investigations to be carried out, or it may lead you into an entirely new branch of magickal growth.

Sample one-day retreat for creating
and empowering a servitor as guardian

Call to adventure:	I'd like to explore the ideas of protective guardians. There have been some major mishaps at home this year, and I feel like the boundaries could use a boost.
Type of focus:	Practice, testing, and trial
Magickal goals:	Create a piece of garden statuary that is actually a protective guardian that watches over house and yard.
Time:	Saturday-all day.
Place:	Home. That's where the servitor will live, so that's where we'll work.
Timing details:	Saturday: a perfect time for protective magicks.
Magickal activities:	Cleanse and charge stones for inclusion in the statue/servitor.
Spiritual activities:	Ritual of naming and empowerment.
Mundane activities:	Lunch; visit to the garden statue store.
Creating mood:	Nothing in particular.
Embracing silence, slowness, and a quiet pace:	Irish dance music in the background. Otherwise, unplugged.
Food:	As needed. Lots of diet cola!
Materials needed:	A garden statue with a hollow base; small quantity of plumber's putty (enough to plug the hole); stones, herbs, and other materials with protective attributes; paper, pen; red thread; reference books; camera; journal; salt; cedar or sweetgrass smudge; matches; Book of Shadows.
Departure:	Nothing in particular. I'll have breakfast and get started.
Schedule:	Saturday morning: Get up, have breakfast. Head for garden statuary stores to purchase the servitor "shell."

Schedule continued:	*Back home: Use resources to help choose correspondences to seal into the statue. Compose a spell or charm of protection, inscribe on a paper scroll, tie with red thread, and tuck into the statue as well. Journal the details and take photos.*
	Once the statue is appropriately "full," plug the hole with putty. Consider a name for the statue.
	Empowering the statue: I will fill it with a projection of my own energy, which can be augmented by drawing energy up from the ground and down from the multiverse. I'll carry out a ritual in which this energy will be instilled and the statue charged, both with energy and with my instructions. I will bless the statue with the four elements: sprinkling with salt and water and smudging. In the final part of the ritual, I'll move the statue to its permanent location—most likely near the front door. I will create a sphere of protection around it, will speak its name aloud, and will assign it its new duties.
	The ritual and the retreat will end here, except for final journaling of the details and final photos. A formal entry in my Book of Shadows will detail the initiation of the servitor's role.
Return:	*Put materials away. The final step will be to make a plan for monitoring the servitor, providing upkeep as needed and renewing the "charge" as needed.*

Notes and Ideas

_____

_____

_____

_____

Suggested Resources for This Chapter

Carlin, Emily. *Defense Against the Dark: A Field Guide to Protecting Yourself from Predatory Spirits, Energy Vampires, and Malevolent Magick.* New Page Books, 2011. (*This wonderful book does triple duty. First, it's a Field Guide for the Dark Arts and Creatures of the Night. Second, it's a manual of core energy practices. And third, it's a compendium of protective magicks.*)

Cuhulain, Kerr. *Magickal Self Defense: A Quantum Approach to Warding.* Llewellyn, 2008. (*An excellent book for learning core energy work and practices.*)

González-Whippler, Migene. *The Complete Book of Amulets and Talismans.* Llewellyn, 1991.

Miller, Jason. *Protection & Reversal Magick: A Witch's Defense Manual.* New Page Books, 2006.

Chapter Twenty

Science and Technomagick Focus

Do you fancy yourself a cybermage? Does much or most of your magickal work or journaling involve the computer? Do you belong to a magickal group or community whose primary existence is digital? Are you interested in digital media or in the intersections between science and magick? If even one of these questions was answered "yes," a retreat that focuses on science or technomagicks could be perfect for you.

Ideas for a retreat focused on science or technomagicks

- Create a cyber Book of Shadows, journal, or other magickal tome.
- Create a ritual space on the Web—i.e., a shrine, a location in Second Life, or the like.
- Design a website.
- Work with document design and/or electronic publication. This could include planning or preparing a book for e-publication.
- Develop and prepare a podcast.
- Study the work of ancient alchemists, or practice working with their symbolic notation.

- Consider modern "metaphorical" or transformational alchemists: for example, soul modification or fire circles.

- Study a modern or arcane science discipline: e.g., quantum physics.

- Work with *mathemagicks* (see the next page):

  - Sacred arithmetic

  - Numerology

  - Sacred geometry and geometry in nature

Sample retreat ideas

1. **Create a digital Book of Shadows, magickal journal, or other sacred text.** Use word processing and/or page design software to create a digital BoS, magickal journal, Book of Write, or other tome on the computer. Your retreat would begin with designing the layout of the book and then move to working with it. Try experimenting with different backgrounds, fonts, and colors.

2. **Design a website.** Use free website software and build a site that allows you to store magickal writings, photographs, blog content, or the like. If you're currently involved in a program of training or apprenticeship, you could use the site to store your materials and make them available to your teacher or mentor. Your site could also be used to publicize and/or sell your writing, artwork, magickal materials, etc.

3. **Create a 'zine for e-publication.** Select a magickal or craft theme and assemble content and images. Be sure to obtain permission if using words or images that belong to someone else. Experiment with and create an overall document design or "look." One by one, plug content into the template and make adjustments as needed. Make your work available to friends or family, or consider selling it through Lulu or another self-publication service.

4. **Work with mathemagicks.** Study sacred geometry and put it to use crafting a labyrinth, henge, or medicine circle. If you have the garden space, make these full-size; if short of space, miniature versions will work as well.

Sample weekend retreat for cybermage heaven and creation of a podcast

Call to adventure:	Everyone is doing podcasts. I don't know much about them, but I want to learn how to do my own.
Type of focus:	Practice, testing, and trial + Seclusion
Magickal goals:	Create and publish a podcast based on a magickal theme.
Time:	Friday evening to Sunday noon.
Place:	Downtown hotel. It's a no-frills hotel, but it has a nice pool and good WiFi.
Timing details:	None, really. I just want to get this done. It's a waxing moon, so that will be useful.
Magickal activities:	Gather information on a controversial magickal topic: "Is a BoS written on a laptop as 'good' as a handwritten BoS?" I will have gathered and recorded several interviews/responses (audio and video) before the retreat
Spiritual activities:	None in particular.
Mundane activities:	Simple foods, maybe a swim or two in the hotel pool.
Creating mood:	Music: alternative, rockabilly.
Embracing silence, slowness, and a quiet pace:	I'll be alone, but the room won't be silent. But I'll be alone.
Food:	Free breakfast at the hotel on Saturday and Sunday. Grab some extra yogurts and pieces of fruit to take back to room. Otherwise, I'm subsisting on pizza, green peppers, and Mountain Dew.

Materials needed:	*Laptop, external (better quality) microphone, homemade pop filter (nylon + embroidery hoop). Everything else needed for podcast (including audio software) is on the computer or available on the Web. Also bring paper, pens, notes, a 12-pack of Mountain Dew, cookies, a few green peppers, pocketknife. NOTE: Before beginning, research the basics of podcasting and make sure all is ready to proceed.*
Departure:	*When I check into my hotel room, I will carry out a brief ritual of beginning and will symbolically turn on my computer and welcome its help as well.*
Schedule:	*The schedule will be rather "loose" and will evolve as needed.* *Friday evening: Pick up a burger on the way to the hotel. Check in around dinnertime. Scarf food. Hold the beginning ritual, power up, and spread out. Get a bucket of ice and chill down MDs and peppers. Begin planning the podcast format: i.e., introductory music, welcome, announcement of theme, presentation of material, and sign-off. (That's highly simplified.) Choose opening music. Begin reviewing and editing recorded interviews.* *Late evening: Go for a swim; grab something from the vending machine on the way back. Return and work some more. Take a bath, go to bed, watch a good film. Eat cookies. Sleep.* *Saturday morning: Up, breakfast in the hotel. Morning swim, shower, and back to work. Continue planning and arranging the podcast plan-aim for no more than 15 minutes. Coffee in room. Develop an outline for the podcast-make a test recording to make sure the volume is correct.* *Lunch: Order pizza to be delivered. Kick back and enjoy. Maybe go for a swim, or check e-mail or Facebook.* *After lunch: Begin recording my clips for the podcast. These, with the recorded interview clips, will make the show. Arrange together using podcasting software. Listen to test run.* *Mid-afternoon: Break from work; swim and cookies.*

Schedule continued:	*Later afternoon: Record audio (much trial and error expected). Convert to MP3 files and prepare to upload to the Web.* *4:30-ish: Order another pizza. (Hot is best!) Throw away the old slices.* *After dinner: Upload podcast to prearranged Web space. Listen to it to assess quality. Set up a Facebook "event" page to announce the podcast. Link to members of the magickal community.* *Evening: Consider and develop a plan for future podcasts. Consider magickal guests, events, topics, and the schedule. Develop a plan for getting feedback back from listeners on podcast #1. What worked, and what didn't?* *Late: Bed!* *Sunday morning: Up early. Check to see if podcast has any feedback. Breakfast in hotel. Pack up and check out.*
Return:	*Head home. Take time to journal (electronically, of course) about the results. What's next? What else do I need to learn to podcast well?*

Notes and Ideas

_____

_____

_____

_____

Suggested Resources for This Chapter

Dunn, Patrick. *Postmodern Magic: The Art of Magic in the Information Age.* Llewellyn, 2005.

Highfield, Roger. *The Science of Harry Potter: How Magic Really Works.* Penguin, 2003.

Roney-Dougal, Serena. *Where Science and Magic Meet.* Green Magick, 2010.

Chapter Twenty-one

Group Retreats

Occasionally, you may find yourself part of a group retreat. As mentioned earlier in this book, there may be times when a magickal group decides to retreat together to accomplish some goal or purpose. Although group retreats are beyond the scope of this book, I wanted to at least mention some of the dynamics.

Groups may choose to retreat for a number of reasons. For instance:

- Those responsible for planning or oversight of an event, group, or activity may meet in one place in order to make plans and finalize arrangements.

- A religious group—like a coven—may choose to retreat together in order to accomplish some sort of magickal work, ritual, or celebration.

- A group overseeing a large undertaking—like a magickal school—may use an annual meeting for ironing out changes in policies, curriculum, setting goals, and so on.

- A group—a class—who are involved in some sort of training or apprenticeship may plan a retreat-getaway akin to a "study group."

- Apprentices or fosterlings may meet together for study, testing, etc.

In general, the same planning components apply to individual and group purposes. One must consider the reason or the need for the retreat as well as considering the overall goals. Without a doubt, the most important measure of success in a group retreat is for each participant to share a common goal and vision. This is absolutely essential in order for the group event to achieve its objectives. If the gathering has ten different individuals going in ten different directions, it's unlikely to be successful and it's *very* likely that it won't end on a good note—i.e., it will end with frustrated and dissatisfied participants.

Specific tips

1. Set the vision. Before the event, hold at least one brainstorming session to generate ideas from the entire group and to figure out the central theme and the key discussion points. Shape these into an agenda and get everyone's approval in advance.

2. Make sure to give each participant a chance to submit their points and concerns. This ensures that everyone's perspectives are considered and also gives each group member a very real sense and stake in what will happen.

3. Once you've accomplished the above steps, prepare a "formal" hard copy agenda and schedule for the meeting.

4. Set guidelines for the event. Decide who is "in charge" or will chair the meeting. Agree on a start and stop time and on the pertinent details.

5. Banish, quash, and be rid of the myth of "Pagan time"! Somehow, somewhere along the line, an unfortunate urban myth took root within the Pagan community. Referred to casually as Pagan Standard Time, or PST, it goes something like this: If you're an hour late for a ritual, circle, class, or other event, you're on time. If you're two hours late, you're still on time. If you don't show up at all, that's okay, too. No one seems sure how or when this mythos got started, but it appears to coincide with the development of the Neo-Pagan movement and may have something to do with a determined effort to veer away from any attempts at structure or organization, which are seen as "mainstream."

    But here's the thing: intentional or careless lateness is rude, pure and simple—and especially so when others are depending on getting something done. If you've gathered people for a specific task, you owe it to them to stay on schedule and get the job done. Assign a participant to be the Lord or Lady of the Schedule, and give him or her the responsibility of keeping the group on time. Ask the schedule keeper to give a fifteen-minute warning before the next agenda item is supposed to begin. In any case, let your group know that the meeting will begin, proceed, and commence according to schedule.

6. Plan a location for the meeting. If people will be staying overnight, plan this, too. You'll need to ensure that everyone has a comfortable place to sleep, along with bedding, towels, and other amenities. Consider places to plug in and charge electronic devices as well as the availability of WiFi.

7. Plan good food, but keep it simple. Having delicious, nutritious food is an important part of group morale and will help keep everyone energized throughout the event. However, you won't want to waste valuable retreat time in the kitchen. Plan on scrumptious food that may be purchased, prepared ahead, or put together quickly. A potluck might be just the thing. Good take-out pizza is another winning idea.

8. Have lots of beverages on hand. Find out everyone's favorite drinks in advance and have a ready supply. Don't forget glasses and ice. Make arrangements to have coffee and hot tea on hand as well.

9. Consider supplies and other needs that might come up during the retreat. For example, you'll almost certainly want wireless access as well as a computer, printer, white board and markers, pads of paper, pens, and other materials.

10. Give some thought to "bling" for the participants. If the group is large or everyone doesn't know each other, you should furnish nametags. You might also want to provide notebooks, carrying bags, mugs, or some other sort of goodie emblazoned with the organization logo, a magickal symbol, or the like. If you're using a printed agenda, this can also be emblazoned with a group image, logo, or sigil.

11. Open *and* close with some sort of group ceremony or ritual, even if brief. This helps draw the group together and reminds everyone of the shared purpose.

12. During the meeting, make sure everyone has a chance to be heard. Some groups benefit from using a "talking stick" (or similar totemic object); this is passed from person to person through the event, and whoever is holding it has the floor. But remember to keep an eye on the schedule. Someone in the group should be responsible for giving "two-minute warnings" or reining in wandering topics when the time limits approach.

   You may want to assign or ask someone to be the discussion moderator. A good moderator will skillfully "quiet" an overly chatty group member (one who is monopolizing the conversation) while also drawing out any especially quiet participants. (Hint: If someone is sitting quietly and not talking, ask him or her a few direct questions—those that can't be answered with "yes" or "no.")

13. Discuss finances well in advance. You may wish to divvy up the various costs and ask everyone to chip in an appropriate share. The organization may be able to contribute to costs as well. Some people may choose to donate funds, supplies, or space and claim a tax write-off.

14. Add to the purpose and intent of your group retreat by giving it a fitting name. There is great power in words, and by matching your intentions to the appropriate name, you'll magnify the event's effectiveness and inspire what happens in the magickal space. Consider the following:

   • **Conclave:** A conclave is a gathering—often private or closed—held for a specific purpose. Conclaves are often used for secret meetings, and particularly for religious functions, as in the sealed Roman conclave that elects a new pope. The word springs from the Latin conclave, meaning "lockable room," from con- "with" + clavis, "key."

   • **Convergence:** This implies a purposeful meeting of those with shared mind and shared purpose. The word's origins are from the Late Latin convergere, meaning "to incline together."

   • **Convocation:** A convocation is an assembly for a formal or ceremonial purpose. The word comes from the Latin convocare, "to call together."

   • Forum: A forum is a place where ideas and views on a particular subject are exchanged. Interestingly, the word springs from Latin roots meaning "what is out of doors," and forums were traditionally held outdoors and in a public area.

- **Gathering:** A festive meeting intended for socialization and enjoyment, often organized around an intended purpose. The focus is on camaraderie, as shown in the roots of the word via the Old English gaderian and related to the Dutch gaderen, "gather together."

- **Moot:** This is an Old English term that derives from the word "meet." It refers to an assembly held for debate or discussion and dates historically to Anglo-Saxon and medieval times. It was also used to describe a regular gathering of people sharing a common interest.

- **Muster:** A gathering of key persons, usually in preparation for a specific undertaking—traditionally prior to a battle or skirmish. The word springs from the Latin monstrare, "to show."

- Salon: A salon is primarily a social gathering by people who share an interest in art, writing, or academic subjects. The salon has its origins in seventeenth-century France, and the French word salon means "large hall."

- **Seminar:** A seminar is a gathering aimed at conference or training; it may also apply to a fixed-term class taught by experts. The word seminar comes from the Latin seminarium, "seed plot," neuter of seminarius, "of seed," from sēmen, "seed." The allusion to a germ of an idea "taking seed" is clear.

- **Summit:** A summit is a meeting attended by the heads of organizations and often by their assistants or underlings as well. The purpose of a summit is to bring representatives from different groups together in order to achieve agreement or understanding on one or more matters. The word derives from the Latin summum, neuter of summus, "highest."

15. Plan some fun, too. The evening after the retreat can be spent sharing dinner and socializing. You could decide to hold a Bardic circle, share a campfire, or spend an evening working with Tarot or other divination tools. You might even watch a magickal film together.

16. Before leaving the event, make sure everyone knows what will happen next. People should be designated to follow up on questions, implement decision

points, and so on. Let everyone know, too, what help is needed to clean up and close down after the meeting.

17. Finally, hold a post-event evaluation. If necessary, arrange for this to be anonymous so that participants can feel free to be honest in their appraisals. Collect and share the results with your original planning group; you can use the feedback in planning the next event.

The Techno-Retreat

In today's technological age, group gatherings may take place partially or fully online. Your group might do all the planning via e-mail or on an Internet forum and then might meet in person for the actual event. If you have one or two members who cannot attend in person, have them join the meeting via Skype, FaceTime, instant messaging, an e-forum, or a telephone conference call. Some groups might choose to conduct the entire meeting online; you can do this through special meeting/seminar software, by conversing through a forum, or by arranging different groups to "Skype" with each other. The Internet makes it possible to bring people in from all over the world.

Notes and Ideas

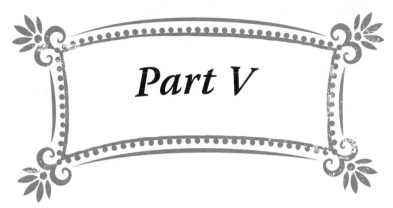

Part V

Afterword

The future belongs to those who believe in the beauty of their dreams.

—ELEANOR ROOSEVELT

There are only two ways of spreading light:
to be the candle or the mirror that reflects it.

—EDITH WHARTON

Chapter Twenty-two

Looking Back...and Ahead

Congratulations, seeker! You've set foot on the path to adventure, entered into "other" space, emerged from a time of testing, and—armed with new knowledge and understanding—returned home. If the retreat has gone well, you're not quite the same person you were when you departed. You may have developed new skills, practiced magicks, engaged in creative work, or done some deep soul-searching. Whatever shape your retreat took, it's important to do a good follow-up evaluation. This not only helps you internalize the process from an objective vantage but also helps you catalog the experience for future reference.

Once you're done evaluating the retreat itself, work through the self-assessment questions below. These will make you think about the changes the experience made in you as well as helping set goals for the months and years to come. To complete these questions, you'll need to look back and consider what you've accomplished, but you'll also need to look forward and think about new goals and new ideas.

Self-Assessment

Having finished your retreat, consider your next steps along the magickal path.

- What would you say is the greatest effect or impression you received from the retreat?

- What are your current needs as a student or practitioner of magick?
- In magickal terms, what is something new that you'd like to try?
- In magickal terms, what is something you'd like to get better at?
- Where would you like to be in your studies, experiences, or training in six months?
- How will you continue to incorporate magick into your everyday life?
- Do you have any ideas for your next retreat? Start writing them down!

I urge you to think through these questions as soon as possible after the retreat ends. The more time that goes by between the retreat and your written evaluation, the more likely you are to forget the details. Capture them early, writing them into your magickal journal and reflecting back on them in the days and weeks to come.

A Fond Farewell . . .

If you skim back through the chapters in this book and the notes you've made, you'll get a sense of the work you've done, how far you've come, and everything you've learned. While you've worked hard at crafting the perfect retreat experience, I also hope you've enjoyed yourself and returned with a sense of peace and rejuvenation. I salute you for your efforts and for your interest in making your magickal life even stronger.

As you contemplate future retreats, please keep an eye on my website. The URL is www.SusanPesznecker.com. I'll be devoting a section of it for sharing resources and ideas for fabulous retreat adventures. I'll also have a spot where those of you who have completed retreats can tell your stories.

For now, I wish you all the best along your path—may you never fear to challenge yourself, and may a new adventure always be waiting...

Part VI

Resources

The guide is definitive. Reality is frequently inaccurate.

—DOUGLAS ADAMS

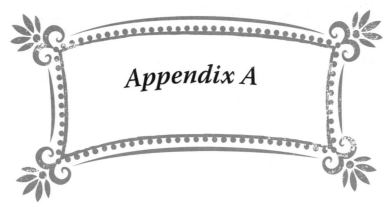

Appendix A

Recommended Readings

The greatest achievement of the human spirit is to live up to one's opportunities and make the most of one's resources.

—MARQUIS DE VAUVENARGUES

In this resource section, you'll find suggested readings and templates for planning your retreats.

Recommended Readings: A Collection of Titles Referenced Throughout This Book

If I could, I'd ask you to read each one of these. It's a wonderful list, and I hope you'll try to work through as many of them as you're able. Just about anything you could use to inspire your retreat is likely to be found in one of the texts below.

Abano, Peter (of). "The Initial Rites and Ceremonies." Sacred-Texts.com. (n.d.) <http://www.sacred-texts.com/grim/bcm/bcm42.htm> (*Includes the tables of planetary hours.*)

Adler, Margo. *Drawing Down the Moon: Witches, Druids, Goddess-Worshippers, and Other Pagans in America.* Penguin, 2006.

Alexander, Jane. *Sacred Rituals at Home.* Sterling, 2000.

Allrich, Karri. *A Witch's Book of Dreams: Understanding the Power of Dreams & Symbols.* Llewellyn, 2001.

Andrews, Ted. *Animal Speak: The Spiritual and Magickal Powers of Creatures Great and Small.* Llewellyn, 1996.

Artress, Lauren. *Walking a Sacred Path: Rediscovering the Labyrinth as a Spiritual Practice.* Riverhead Trade, 2006.

Baker, Nick. *The Amateur Naturalist.* National Geographic, 2005.

Bardey, Catherine. *Secrets of the Spas: Pamper and Vitalize Yourself at Home.* Black Dog & Leventhal, 1999.

Bennett, Robin Rose. *Healing Magic: A Green Witch Guidebook.* Sterling, 2004.

Bonewits, Isaac, and Philip Carr-Gomm. *Bonewits' Essential Guide to Druidism.* Citadel, 2006.

Brunvand, Jan. *The Study of American Folklore, 4th edition.* Norton, 1998.

Buckland, Raymond. *Buckland's Complete Book of Witchcraft.* Llewellyn, 2002. (*A look at Gardnerian-influenced Wicca for the beginner.*)

Campbell, Joseph. *The Hero with a Thousand Faces.* New World Library, 2008. (*Campbell's seminal writing on the monomyth and the hero's journey.*)

Campbell, Joseph, and Bill Moyers. *The Power of Myth.* Anchor, 1991. (*Campbell's work on the importance of mythos through world cultures.*)

Carlin, Emily. *Defense Against the Dark: A Field Guide to Protecting Yourself from Predatory Spirits, Energy Vampires, and Malevolent Magick.* New Page Books, 2011. (*This wonderful book does triple duty. First, it's a Field Guide for the Dark Arts and Creatures of the Night. Second, it's a manual of core energy practices. And third, it's a compendium of protective magicks.*)

Conway, D. J. *Moon Magick: Myth & Magic, Crafts & Recipes, Rituals & Spells.* Llewellyn, 2002.

Cuhulain, Kerr. *Magickal Self Defense: A Quantum Approach to Warding.* Llewellyn, 2008. (*An excellent book for learning core energy work and practices.*)

———. *Modern Knighthood: Unleashing Your Inner Warrior to Master Yourself and Your World.* Smashwords (e-book), 2010.

Cunningham, Scott. *The Complete Book of Incense, Oils, and Brews.* Llewellyn, 2002.

———. *Cunningham's Encyclopedia of Crystal, Gem, and Metal Magick.* Llewellyn, 1998.

———. *Earth Power: Techniques of Natural Magic.* Llewellyn, 2002.

Daimler, Morgan. *By Land, Sea, and Sky: A Selection of Repaganized Prayers and Charms from Volumes 1 & 2 of the Carmina Gadelica.* Lulu, 2010.

Dalai Lama (His Holiness the). *365: Daily Advice from the Heart.* ThorsonElement, 2001. (*A wonderful little book of daily meditations.*)

Dinwiddie, Robert, et al. *Universe.* DK Adult, 2008.

Drew, A. J. *A Wiccan Formulary and Herbal.* New Page Books, 2004.

Dugan, Ellen. *Garden Witch's Herbal: Green Magick, Herbalism & Spirituality.* Llewellyn, 2009.

Dunn, Patrick. *Postmodern Magic: The Art of Magic in the Information Age.* Llewellyn, 2005.

Ellison, Rev. Robert Lee "Skip." *Ogham: The Secret Language of the Druids.* ADF Publishing, 2008.

Emery, Carla. *The Encyclopedia of Country Living.* Sasquatch, 2008. (*A compendium of the domestic arts of self-sufficiency.*)

Gallagher, Ann-Marie. *The Spells Bible: The Definitive Guide to Charms and Enchantments.* Sterling, 2003.

———. *The Wicca Bible: The Definitive Guide to Magic and the Craft.* Sterling, 2005.

Gelb, Michael J. *How to Think Like Leonardo da Vinci.* Delta, 2004. (*A wonderful book that explains da Vinci's seven-step explanation of intentional learning, creativity, and personal growth.*)

George, Demetra, and Douglas Birch. *Astrology for Yourself: How to Understand and Interpret Your Own Birth Chart.* Ibis, 2006. (*An excellent introductory text for those new to astrology, but detailed enough for the experienced user as well.*)

González-Whippler, Migene. *The Complete Book of Amulets and Talismans.* Llewellyn, 1991.

Greer, John Michael. *Pagan Prayer Beads: Magic and Meditation with Pagan Rosaries.* Weiser, 2007.

Hall, Manly K. *The Secret Teachings of All Ages.* Wilder, 2009. (*A gorgeous book, filled with the arcane knowledge of the ages and illustrated with striking full-color plates.*)

Harris, Eleanor, and Philip Harris. *The Crafting & Use of Ritual Tools: Step-by-Step Instructions for Woodcrafting Religious & Magical Implements.* Llewellyn, 2002.

Henes, Donna. *Celestially Auspicious Occasions: Seasons, Cycles, & Celebrations.* Perigee, 1996.

Highfield, Roger. *The Science of Harry Potter: How Magic Really Works.* Penguin, 2003.

Illes, Judika. *Element Encyclopedia of Witchcraft.* Thorsons, 2005. (*An encyclopedic work by Illes; this one focuses on different elements of craft, correspondences, etc.*)

———. *Encyclopedia of 5000 Spells.* HarperOne, 2009. (*Another encyclopedic tome of spellcraft, components, and so forth.*)

Jordan, Michael. *Ceremonies for Life.* Collins and Brown, 2001.

Judith, Anodea. *Chakra Balancing.* Sounds True, 2006.

Jung, C. G. *The Red Book.* Norton, 2009.

K, Amber. *Ritual Craft: Creating Rites for Transformation and Celebration.* Llewellyn, 2006.

Leslie, Clare Walker and Charles E. Roth. *Keeping a Nature Journal: Discover a Whole New Way of Seeing the World Around You.* Storey, 2003.

Lippincott, Kristen. *Astronomy (DK Eyewitness Books).* DK Children, 2008. (*An image-rich guide that provides a wonderful introduction to astronomy.*)

Llewellyn's Sabbats Almanac. Llewellyn, published annually.

Maresh, Jan Saunders. *Sewing for Dummies, 3rd edition.* Wiley, 2010.

MacLir, Alferian Gwydion. *Wandlore: The Art of Crafting the Ultimate Magical Tool.* Llewellyn, 2011.

Miller, Jason. *Protection & Reversal Magick: A Witch's Defense Manual.* New Page Books, 2006.

Moore, Barbara. *Tarot for Beginners: A Practical Guide to Reading the Cards.* Llewellyn, 2010.

Mosley, Ivo, ed. *Earth Poems: Poems from Around the World to Honor the Earth.* HarperSanFrancisco, 1996.

Moura, Ann. *Green Witchcraft III: The Manual.* Llewellyn, 2000.

Ophir, Eyal, Clifford Nass, and Anthony D. Wagner. "Cognitive Control in Media Multitaskers." Proceedings of the National Academy of Sciences. July, 2009. http://www.scribd.com/doc/19081547/Cognitive-control-in-media-multitaskers

Paxson, Diana L. *Taking Up the Runes: A Complete Guide to Using Runes in Spells, Rituals, Divination, and Magic.* Weiser, 2005.

Pellant, Chris. *Rocks and Minerals (Smithsonian Handbook).* DK Adult, 2002.

Pesznecker, Susan. *Crafting Magick with Pen and Ink: Learn to Write Stories, Spells, and Other Magickal Works.* Llewellyn, 2009.

Peterson Field Guides. Houghton Mifflin Harcourt, various years. (*These pocket guides are available for every type of natural observation—birds, trees, weather, herbs, etc.— and for many specific geological areas, too.*)

Pollan, Michael. "Michael Pollan." 2011. http://michaelpollan.com/ (*Pollan is one of America's preeminent food scholars and journalists and has written several books about food and food culture. His site includes many of his essays and writings.*)

Regardie, Israel, and Pat Zalewski. *Ceremonial Magic: A Guide to the Mechanisms of Ritual.* Aeon, 2008.

Roberts, Elizabeth, and Elias Amidon, eds. *Life Prayers: 365 Prayers, Blessings, and Affirmations to Celebrate the Human Journey.* HarperSanFrancisco, 1996.

Roney-Dougal, Serena. *Where Science and Magic Meet.* Green Magick, 2010.

Scarpa, Sandra McCraw. *Magical Fabric Art: Spellwork & Wishcraft through Patchwork Quilting and Sewing.* Llewellyn, 1998.

Serith, Ceisiwr. *A Book of Pagan Prayer.* Weiser, 2002. (*A lovely collection of Pagan-oriented prayers and blessings for all occasions from the casual to the celebratory.*)

Smedley, Wendy. *Start Scrapbooking: Your Essential Guide to Recording Memories.* Memory Makers, 2010.

Sommer, Robin Langley. *Nota Bene: A Guide to Familiar Latin Quotes and Phrases.* Barnes and Noble, 1995.

Starhawk. *The Spiral Dance: A Rebirth of the Ancient Religion of the Goddess, 20th Anniversary Edition.* HarperOne, 1999.

Sullivan, Tammy. *Elemental Witch: Fire, Air, Water, Earth; Discover Your Natural Affinity.* Llewellyn, 2006.

Telesco, Patricia. *A Kitchen Witch's Cookbook.* Llewellyn, 2002.

———. *Exploring Candle Magick.* Career, 2008.

The Old Farmer's Almanac. Old Farmer's Almanac, published annually.

We'Moon: Gaia Rhythms for Womyn. Mother Tongue Ink, 2011. (*Published continually since 1980, this annual combines a datebook format with art, poetry, readings, moon lore, and astrology. Although decidedly woman-centered, it is full of wonderful magick and interpersonal insights that anyone could use.*)

Zell-Ravenheart, Oberon. *Companion for the Apprentice Wizard.* New Page Books, 2004. (*A detail-packed sequel to Zell-Ravenheart's Grimoire.*)

———. *Green Egg Omelette: An Anthology of Art and Articles from the Legendary Pagan Journal.* New Page Books, 2008.

———. *Grimoire for the Apprentice Wizard.* New Page Books, 2004. (*This book, which has been described as a "Boy Scout Handbook for magick users," is rich with "how-tos" and tables of correspondences, planetary hours, rituals, spellwork, and the like.*)

Zell-Ravenheart, Oberon, and Morning Glory Zell-Ravenheart. *Creating Circles and Ceremonies: Rituals for All Seasons and Reasons.* New Page Books, 2006.

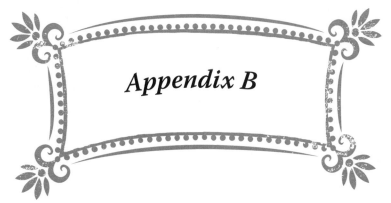

Appendix B

Templates for Your Retreat

Template for Retreat Planning

Call to adventure:	
Type of Focus	
Magickal goals:	
Time:	
Place:	
Timing details:	
Magickal activities:	

Spiritual activities:	
Mundane activities:	
Creating mood:	
Embracing silence, slowness, and a quiet pace:	
Food:	
Materials needed:	
Departure (more on this in chapter 8):	

Schedule:	
Return (more on this in chapter 9):	

Retreat Journal Template

Use this if you're new to journaling, don't currently have a magickal journal, or want something special just for this activity.

Journal entry	
Date:	Day of week:
Moon phase:	
Mood:	
Notes:	

Trip Plan Template

Make a copy of this page, fill out the copy, and make two more copies of the completed version. Give one copy to a friend, neighbor, or family member; post one copy on your refrigerator; and tuck the original into your purse or wallet.

Trip plan for [name]:
I am headed to this location:
I am leaving at _____ on _____.
I will return at _____ on _____.
Mode of travel (car, plane, or others, with details):
Travel information (road directions, flight number, arrival times, and other important details):
In case of emergency, contact me at:
In case of emergency, contact _____ at:
Other information:

Appendix C

Magickal Resources for Your Retreat

If you can DREAM it, you can DO it.
—WALT DISNEY

The following materials are ready for you to pluck-and-drop into your retreat plans. Or, use them to inspire your own spells, charms, and rituals.

Safe Travel Charm

Fill a small drawstring bag (or knot together a piece of fabric) with stones, herbs, runes, or other items that correspond with protection and guidance (e.g., jade, quartz, snowflake obsidian, sage, sweetgrass, a protective rune such as *Algiz*). Repeat the following:

> *I fill the bag for travel safe,*
> *May magickal powers guide me.*
> *Journey smoothly to your place,*
> *The Goddess' arms around me.*

Keep the charm with you as you travel.

A second charm:

> *As I travel from this place,*
> *Keep me wrapped in sacred space.*
> *Safe my journey, smooth and swift,*
> *My guardians' care a precious gift.*

Purification Shower or Bath

Shower as usual, using an herbed soap good for purification, such as frankincense. When finished, dip in and out of the shower three times, reciting the following:

[First dip] *I am washing away fatigue, despair, and ill health.*

[Second dip] *I am purifying myself with waters from the living cauldron.*

[Third dip] *I am cloaking myself with blessings and living protection.*

Note: If you bathed instead of showering, dip your head underwater as you repeat the above. Or, turn on the shower and use it to complete the ritual.

General Blessing

> *Life grows more radiant about me.*
> *Life grows more arduous for me.*
> *Life grows more abundant within me.*
> —RUDOLF STEINER

Morning Blessings

> *Another day,*
> *Here for me—*
> *Greet the morning,*
> *Blessed be!*

> *A boon is given this morning—*
> *A new day, full of potential.*
> *May I be worthy of this gift.*

Blessing Over Food

I take this food
With gratitude.
May it nourish me—
So shall it be!

To earth and sky,
To fertile ground,
I offer thanks
For bounty found.

Ways to Begin

Choose one and use it to open ritual, blessings, or other magickal workings:

Thus it begins.
So mote it be.
So shall it be.
I declare it so.
I declare it open.
May it be true.
May it be so.
And so I begin.
And so it begins.

Invocation

Creator, I stand at the start of a journey.
Many discoveries and tests await.
I have learned much with your help; now my steps must be my own.
May I remember your teachings, your patience, and your wisdom.
May my steps be sure and my confidence strong.
May the journey take me to new understandings.
May my growth know no bounds.

Be here, now.
Be here, always.

Rituals of Beginning

First ritual

You'll need your retreat materials; an altar cloth: consider red (for passion and energy), green (creativity and prosperity), or yellow (mental work); a small dish of salt; a feather or bit of ribbon; a candle; matches; a small dish of water; your own personal indications of deity (or a simple white taper); a small thurible for burning herbs or incense; incense or loose herbs; a candlesnuffer (or silver spoon); additional items that honor your goals; cakes and wine.

"Today I set myself upon a _____ path." [Fill in according to your needs or intentions.]

"I ask blessings and strength of earth. [Sprinkle a few grains of salt over your altar or materials.] *May vigor and perseverance be mine."*

"I ask blessings and strength of air. [Waft the feather over your altar or materials.] *May inspiration and mystery be mine."*

"I ask blessings and strength of fire. [Waft the candle's "smoke" over your altar or materials.] *May passion and creativity be mine."*

"I ask blessings and strength of water. [Sprinkle a drop or two of water over your altar or materials.] *May energy and transformation be mine."*

"May the spirit of the hero's journey fill me, gifting me with powers of insight and creation. May the spirit empower my purpose, enlivening these materials to my purpose." [Alternatively, address your own deities as you see fit.]

[Light thurible, if using. As smoke forms, use your hands to waft the smoke over your body.] *"May the life-power of these herbs bestow their blessing upon me."* [If using dry herbs without burning, sprinkle a few over your head.]

[Lay hands on magickal tools.] *"In return for these gifts, I do hereby pledge to honor my craft and that I will devote myself to it and celebrate the traditions and ways of my path."*

[Pause for a minute or two of quiet meditation.]

"The circle is open. So mote it be."

[Pause for a moment of reflection. Enjoy cakes and wine. Allow the candles to burn out or snuff, giving thanks.]

Second Ritual of Beginning—Including Creation of Sacred Space

Use tools or materials as desired. This very simple opening can be performed without any props.

Spirits of the east, place of air, hall of winds, hear me!
Spirits of the south, place of fire, crucible of the rising sun, hear me!
Spirits of the west, place of water, cauldron of the greatest ocean, hear me!
Spirits of the north, place of earth, panticle of stone, hear me!

The circle is cast. I am within sacred space, between the worlds. [This is a good time to ring a bell if you have one.]

Third Ritual of Beginning

Cast a circle, working with wand or hand. Before beginning, repeat, *Magick brings the circle round, twines the worlds, forever bound.*

Call the quarters, beginning with the east and working deosil (sun-wise, or clockwise).
Direct wand to the east and repeat: *Spirits of the east, home of winds, be welcome.*
South: *Spirits of the south, home of fire and forge, be welcome.*
West: *Spirits of the west, home of waters of life, be welcome.*
North: *Spirits of the north, home of earthen stone, be welcome.*

Give your statement of purpose and intention. Repeat the following invocation: *Great spirit,* a needy one stands before you. Guide me now as I enter this retreat for a good and sacred purpose.*

*If you choose, substitute one or more specific deities or patrons.

The magick begins—I am within all realms.

Kindling Fire

When kindling fire, use carefully selected woods that are sacred to you. Arrange the fire in advance: crumbled paper, old bits of candles, or laundry lint should be loosely piled in the center. Build a mound of twigs and thin burnables around the core, leaving one side open for lighting. Stand thumb-thick sticks around the core, teepee style. Add slightly larger sticks, building up to larger pieces of seasoned firewood. This kind of a teepee fire lights quickly and burns quickly, making it a great ritual fire. For extra sturdiness, lay four large pieces of wood in a square surrounding the teepee; this will brace the teepee and the large pieces will also gradually catch fire and may be pushed in toward the center of the fire pit for a steady blaze.

In my family, sacred words are spoken aloud when a campfire or ritual fire is lit, and it is considered a mark of honor that the fire light successfully on the first try.

Ritual of the Ashes

Every time you burn candles, herbs, incense, or a campfire, save a bit of the ashes or soot. Add these remnants to a jar, and keep a list of when the ashes were added, where they came from, the dates, and the circumstances.

Whenever you kindle a new fire, sprinkle in some of the saved ashes. After the fire is done and cooled, scoop up a bit, add back to the jar, update your list, and so forth.

As your jar of ashes accumulates, they become a powerful addition to both fire and sympathetic magick. Your retreat provides a great time to begin your own Ritual of the Ashes.

Ritual of Naming

Old ones:
You have delivered me a name, and I accept it with gratitude.
Hereafter, I shall be called _____.
Let me say this again: [Repeat the naming three times.]
> *My name is _____.*
> *My name is _____.*
> *My name is _____.*
I go forth, bearing this name. May I honor and be worthy of it.

Ways to Finish

Choose one and use it to close ritual, blessings, or other magickal workings:
> *Thus it ends.*
> *So mote it be.*

So shall it be.
I declare it so.
I declare it closed.
May it be with me always.
May it always be so.
May it end here.
Forever and always.
And so it ends.

Ritual of Ending or Leaving

Standing at the altar, hold in your hands (or set on the altar) symbols of your successful quest.

Repeat the following: *Ashes to ashes, dust to dust, all returns to Creator, as it must.*

Recall the quarters/watchtowers/guardians/elementals as desired.

Place your hands on your retreat's "work" or results and repeat: *This journey is complete. By earth, air, fire, water, these works are consecrated to purpose and intention. May I see continued growth and benefit from this journey. May I continue to travel a true path. May I be unafraid of the challenges that await me in the future. I go now, in peace and greater understanding.*

Release the elements beginning with north and working widdershins (counterclockwise). *Spirits of north, west, south, and east, merry part, and I thank you for your guardianship.*

Benediction: *May the Creator-source continue to gift me with vitality. May Father Sun and Mother Moon shine down their bounties of beauty and illumination. May the four winds bear seeds of inspiration and an always-changing view. May I grow strong in the ongoing presence of the Shining Ones. May I go now, in peace.*

Alternate/optional release with extinguishing of candles, if used: *I bless and release the protection of spirit* [snuff the deity candle], *water, fire* [snuff the fire candle], *air, and earth* [snuff other candles and put a lid over the thurible]. *Let us go in peace.*

Another optional release: *Grateful blessings, oh spirits of west, south, east, and north. You have graced me with your wisdom. Go now, in peace and bounty, until we should meet anew.*

Blessings for Inspiration

Here within this space I weave
A work of mental clarity.
Through open channels I aspire
To kindle psychic inner fire.

Gift my head with wisdom,
My eyes with clarity,
My ears with alertness,
My mouth with tact,
My hands with skill,
My heart with patience,
My feet with strength,
My soul with courage.
May this be so!

Blessings for the Natural World

Bless this world,
Earth, air, water, fire,
Spirit above,
Spirit below,
Home to all.
May we nurture, love,
Bless this world.

I went to the woods because I wanted to live deliberately. I wanted to live deep and
suck out all the marrow of life. To put to rout all that was not life and not when I
had come to die discover that I had not lived.
—HENRY DAVID THOREAU

Charm of Manifestation

By all the powers of earth and sea,
By all the might of moon and sun,

As I do will, so mote it be;
Chant the spell and it be done!
Blessed be!

Charm for Cleansing

Use these separately or together:

Water, salt, where you are cast,
No ill or adverse purpose last.
Evil spirits all must flee;
As I do will, so mote it be!

Through smoke and fire I purify
No evil shall remain nearby.
Cleansed of harm and ill are ye,
As is my will, so mote it be!

Moon Blessing

Gentle moon, silver beacon,
Clarity of sharp vision,
Gift me with the magick of your shining light.

Useful Latin Phrases and Quotations for "Special Effects"

Working in a language other than English can add a sense of mysticism and elegance to one's magickal working, and if you're fluent in a second language, by all means use it to embellish your workings. Using Latin is especially engaging as so much of our language springs from Latin roots; working with Latin thus becomes a nice way to recall and forge those ancient connections.

Below I offer a group of Latin phrases that you may find useful in your retreat experience, whether using them in ritual or spellwork, inscribing them into a journal, or simply finding inspiration in their meaning.

Alea iacta est: "The die is cast." This would be a good ending—i.e., something to offer at the end of a spell, or after a period of divination. This would be fun, too, for its theatrical intention. If working with a bonfire, it would be a perfect time to scatter a bit of magickal or colored powder over the flames for effect.

De mortuis nil nisi bonum: "Let nothing but good concerning (be said of) the dead." A fine bit for honoring ancestors or Shining Ones; would also be excellent for certain occasions, such as Samhain, or rituals held in the winter.

Ex amino: "From the heart, sincerely." This could be used in many ways, including as part of the invocation, a welcoming, as a codicil to the magickal workings, or as a closing benediction.

In Terra veritas: "In the Earth, truth." As someone highly in tune with green magick, I can see using this in a number of ways, including before or after grounding, spellcraft, and meditations or when planting or honoring trees, plants, stones, or other natural objects. It would also work well in rituals honoring the Wheel of the Year or in any Earth-centered magick.

Multum in parvo: "Much in a little." Another powerful addition to all kinds of spellwork, where our workings are small emblems of a hoped-for larger result. I could also imagine using this in herbology, especially when crafting an herbal remedy or potion. A small bit of dried herbs can work magick!

Noli me tangere: "Touch me not, let nothing touch me" or (loosely) "Do not interfere." A great invocation to accompany grounding, centering, and especially shielding, as well as spells of banishing or protection.

Summum bonum: "The supreme good" or "the highest good." An excellent way to open or close either ritual or spellwork.

Nil sine numini: "Nothing without providence." Excellent for supporting ritual or spellwork, as well as (specifically) for spells involving wealth or prosperity.

Amor omnes vincent: "Love conquers all."

Tempus fugit: "Time flies."

Ars longis; vita brevis: "Art is long; life is short."

Per ardua ad astra! "Through struggle to the stars!"

Sic transit gloria mundi: "Thus passes the glories of the world."

Bene vixit qui bene latuit: "One lives best by the hidden life."

Omnia vivunt, omnia inter se conexa: "Everything is alive, everything is interconnected."

Omnia in arte magica est: "All is in the magick."

Semper crescens semper discentes: "Always growing always learning."

Tam supra, quam subter:"As above, so below."

Tam intra, quam extra: "As within, so without."

Quid credes, sic est: "What thou believest, so it is."

Ipsa scientia potestas est: "Knowledge itself is power."

Cum potestate magna rationem reddere convenit: "With great power comes great responsibility."

Quisquis circumit, evenit: "What goes around, comes around."

Scientia et sapientia: "Knowledge and wisdom."

Suggested Resources for This Appendix

Conway, D. J. *Moon Magick: Myth & Magic, Crafts & Recipes, Rituals & Spells.* Llewellyn, 2002.

K, Amber. *Ritual Craft: Creating Rites for Transformation and Celebration.* Llewellyn, 2006.

Pesznecker, Susan. *Crafting Magick with Pen and Ink: Learn to Write Stories, Spells, and Other Magickal Works.* Llewellyn, 2009.

We'Moon: Gaia Rhythms for Womyn. Mother Tongue Ink, 2011. (*Published continually since 1980, this annual combines a datebook format with art, poetry, readings, moon lore, and astrology. Although decidedly woman-centered, it is full of wonderful magick and interpersonal insights that anyone could use.*)

Zell-Ravenheart, Oberon. *Grimoire for the Apprentice Wizard.* New Page Books, 2004. (*This book, which has been described as a "Boy Scout Handbook for magick users," is rich with "how-tos" and tables of correspondences, planetary hours, rituals, spellwork, and the like.*)

Zell-Ravenheart, Oberon, and Morning Glory Zell-Ravenheart. *Companion for the Apprentice Wizard.* New Page Books, 2004. (*A detail-packed sequel to Zell-Ravenheart's Grimoire.*)

———. *Creating Circles and Ceremonies: Rituals for All Seasons and Reasons.* New Page Books, 2006.

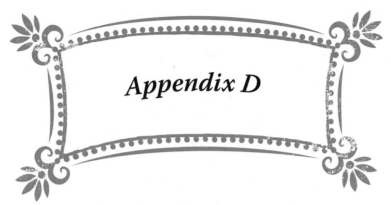

About the Mentors
Quoted in This Book

If a man could pass through Paradise in a dream,
and have a flower presented to him as a pledge
that his soul had really been there,
and if he found that flower in his hand when he awoke,
—Ay! And what then?

—SAMUEL TAYLOR COLERIDGE, *ANIMA POETAE*

When I see people quoted in books and writings, I always wonder why they were chosen. So, I thought I'd tell you a little bit about why I chose the people who are quoted in the book and particularly why so many "non-magickal" folks are being quoted in a book about magick. What it boils down to is that I really don't draw lines between magickal and non-magickal. Magick is all around us: that's a fact. We're swimming in it. Some of us realize that, and some don't—but we're all affected by it nonetheless. When I find quotations that strike me as moving or important or in some way worthy, I assume that they have been inspired by the magick of the multiverse whether or not the speaker realizes it.

The quotations used in this work were selected because I thought they were *just right* for the moment. When I went to put together the mini-bios of their speakers, I was surprised at the variety of paths, times, and backgrounds that came up. I like them a lot, and I hope you enjoy them, too.

Douglas Adams: A twentieth-century English writer and dramatist, Adams is best known for his *Hitchhiker's Guide to the Galaxy.* He was also deeply involved with the environmental movement, in particular advocating for endangered animals.

George Gordon Byron (a.k.a. Lord Byron): A nineteenth-century English romantic poet. One of Byron's most important contributions to poetry was his use of the "Byronic hero," an archetypal figure seen throughout much of his writing and later adopted as a trope by other writer's and poets. [*Note: Byron's hero perfectly fits Joseph Campbell's hero monomyth.*]

Joseph Campbell: A twentieth-century American scholar specializing in comparative mythology and comparative religions, Campbell is especially well-known for his work with the monomyth and the hero's journey. The tropes he identified pervade modern literature, art, dance, and film.

Lewis Carroll (a.k.a. Charles Lutwidge Dodgson): A nineteenth-century English writer, mathematician, and photographer, Carroll is best remembered for his *Alice's Adventures in Wonderland.* His work played with the mind and introduced elements of fantasy in a way largely (at that time) unexplored in the field.

Samuel Taylor Coleridge: A nineteenth-century English poet who, with John Keats, is said to have founded the Romantic movement. His often-fantastical work is known for expecting readers to "suspend disbelief."

Helen Cordes: A modern American writer who explores ideas of cultural transformation. She authors the national bimonthly periodical *New Moon Girls.*

Walt Disney: A twentieth-century American filmmaker, visionary, and philanthropist, Disney was famous for his visions of possibility and enjoying life. He not only created the Disney empire but also the world's most famous animated character: Mickey Mouse.

Benjamin Disraeli: A nineteenth-century English politician and writer who served two terms as Great Britain's prime minister. His writing was known for its social and political commentary.

Albert Einstein: A twentieth-century German-born physicist who discovered/ explained the general theory of relativity and the specific relationships between mass and energy. Einstein escaped Nazi Germany in the years before World War II, came to the U.S., and became an American citizen. He is known for intellect, perseverance, curiosity, and a refusal to allow obstacles to stand in his way. Today, Einstein's work continues to hold up even as scientists probe the bounds of quantum mechanics, the place where some suspect magick and science might intersect.

Ralph Waldo Emerson: A nineteenth-century American poet and philosopher, Emerson was a main player in developing the Transcendental movement. He believed strongly in individuality and freedom and placed immense value in lessons and experiences gleaned from nature.

Johann Wolfgang von Goethe: A German literary figure and scientist who lived from 1749 until 1832, Goethe is known for his classic romantic literature and poetry. His *Faust* stands as possibly the greatest full-length modern heroic poem. His dense works inspired artistic movements throughout Europe.

Sir Edmund Hillary: A twentieth-century mountaineer and explorer from New Zealand, Hillary is known for making the first ascent of Mt. Everest. He was known for his zest for living, intense curiosity, and the belief that human potential was boundless.

Ursula K. Le Guin: A beloved modern American author, Le Guin writes seminal science fiction that breaks the bounds of old forms and integrates modern issues—politics, feminism, ethnic conflict. Her well-known works include the *Earthsea* series and the prize-winning *The Left Hand of Darkness.*

Molière (a.k.a. Jean-Baptiste Poquelin): A seventeenth-century French playwright, considered to be one of modern literature's most important comedic voices. Many of the terms and descriptions he coined for comedic elements remain in use today and are considered canonical.

Eden Phillpotts: A twentieth-century English author, born in India during the nineteenth century. A prolific writer, poet, and dramatist, Phillpotts wrote intensely human stories and set many of them in the picturesque English countryside. The countryside was of supreme importance to him; he was deeply involved in conservation groups and supported preservation of the natural world.

Plato: A student of Socrates, Plato lived in the fourth century BCE. He was a philosopher-scholar and had a key role in establishing the traditional disciplines of education and science. Plato's "Allegory of the Cave" holds up as an example of *how* the human mind approaches a problem.

Eleanor Roosevelt: One of America's first ladies (her husband was Franklin Delano Roosevelt), Eleanor Roosevelt was well known for her work in civil rights, human rights (she was a United Nations delegate for thirteen years), and the advancement of women's rights. She was much beloved for her support of the American people through World War II.

Socrates: A classical Greek philosopher, Socrates is acknowledged as one of the founders of the fields of Western philosophy and ethics. Throughout his life, he emphasized the need for self-evaluation and the search for truth. His constant self-examination—as well as the examination of others—led to what we know today as the "Socratic method."

Rudolf Steiner: An Austrian philosopher and esoteric thinker who lived from 1861 until 1925, Steiner was a cultural philosopher who founded the movement known as Anthroposophy. His work attempted to merge science and mysticism; he used the results to try and meet the spiritual needs of his fellow human beings. Among other things, he is known for his work in Waldorf education and the field of biodynamic farming.

Henry David Thoreau: A nineteenth-century American philosopher and transcendentalist, Thoreau is regarded as an early environmentalist who saw the natural world as seminal to the human condition.

Vincent Van Gogh: A nineteenth-century Dutch painter famous for his work with vivid colors and for planting strong emotions into his work, Van Gogh always pushed himself to new extremes. Suffering throughout his life with often debilitating emotional illness, Van Gogh embodied hard work and personal challenge.

Marquis de Vauvenargues (a.k.a. Luc de Clapiers): An eighteenth-century French writer and ethicist, known for his explorations into moral philosophy and literary criticism.

Earl Warren: A twentieth-century lawyer, politician, and the fourteenth Supreme Court Chief Justice of the United States, Warren was known for legislation that supported and advanced human rights and social progress.

Edith Wharton: A Pulitzer prize-winning American novelist and poet. Writing at the turn of the twentieth century, Wharton's work often focused on social and cultural commentary. She was particularly interested in the expansion of the role of women in society.

Bibliography

Abano, Peter (of). "The Initial Rites and Ceremonies." Sacred-Texts.com. (n.d.) <http://www.sacred-texts.com/grim/bcm/bcm42.htm> (*Includes the tables of planetary hours.*)

Adler, Margo. *Drawing Down the Moon: Witches, Druids, Goddess-Worshippers, and Other Pagans in America.* New York: Penguin, 2006.

Alexander, Jane. *Sacred Rituals at Home.* New York: Sterling, 2000.

Allrich, Karri. *A Witch's Book of Dreams: Understanding the Power of Dreams & Symbols.* Llewellyn, 2001.

Andrews, Ted. *Animal Speak: The Spiritual and Magickal Powers of Creatures Great and Small.* St. Paul, MN: Llewellyn, 1996.

Artress, Lauren. *Walking a Sacred Path: Rediscovering the Labyrinth as a Spiritual Practice.* New York: Riverhead Trade, 2006.

Baker, Nick. *The Amateur Naturalist.* Washington, D.C.: National Geographic, 2005.

Bardey, Catherine. *Secrets of the Spas: Pamper and Vitalize Yourself at Home.* New York: Black Dog & Leventhal, 1999.

Bennett, Robin Rose. *Healing Magic: A Green Witch Guidebook.* New York: Sterling, 2004.

Bonewits, Isaac and Philip Carr-Gomm. *Bonewits' Essential Guide to Druidism.* New York: Citadel, 2006.

Brunvand, Jan. *The Study of American Folklore (4th Ed).* New York: Norton, 1998.

Buckland, Raymond. *Buckland's Complete Book of Witchcraft.* St. Paul, MN: Llewellyn, 2002. (*A look at Gardnerian-influenced Wicca for the beginner.*)

Campbell, Joseph. *The Hero with a Thousand Faces.* Novato, CA: New World Library, 2008. First published in 1949 by Pantheon Books. (*Campbell's seminal writing on the monomyth and the hero's journey.*)

Campbell, Joseph, and Bill Moyers. *The Power of Myth.* New York: Anchor, 1991. (*Campbell's work on the importance of mythos through world cultures.*)

Carlin, Emily. *Defense Against the Dark: A Field Guide to Protecting Yourself from Predatory Spirits, Energy Vampires, and Malevolent Magick.* Pompton Plains, NJ: New Page Books, 2011. (*This wonderful book does triple duty. First, it's a field guide for the Dark Arts and Creatures of the Night. Second, it's a manual of core energy practices. And third, it's a compendium of protective magicks.*)

Conway, D. J. *Moon Magick: Myth & Magic, Crafts & Recipes, Rituals & Spells.* St. Paul, MN: Llewellyn, 2002.

Cuhulain, Kerr. *Magickal Self Defense: A Quantum Approach to Warding.* Woodbury, MN: Llewellyn, 2008. (*An excellent book for learning core energy work and practices.*)

———. *Modern Knighthood: Unleashing Your Inner Warrior to Master Yourself and Your World.* Los Gatos, CA: Smashwords (e-book; www.smashwords.com/), 2010.

Cunningham, Scott. *Cunningham's Encyclopedia of Crystal, Gem, and Metal Magick.* Llewellyn, 1998.

———. *Earth Power: Techniques of Natural Magic.* St. Paul, MN: Llewellyn, 2002.

———. *The Complete Book of Incense, Oils, and Brews.* St. Paul, MN: Llewellyn, 2002.

Daimler, Morgan. *By Land, Sea, and Sky: A Selection of Repaganized Prayers and Charms from Volumes 1 & 2 of the Carmina Gadelica.* Raleigh, NC: Lulu, 2010.

Dalai Lama (His Holiness the). *365: Daily Advice from the Heart.* London: Thorsons Element, 2001. (*A wonderful little book of daily meditations.*)

Dinwiddie, Robert, et al. *Universe.* New York: DK Adult, 2008.

Drew, A. J. *A Wiccan Formulary and Herbal.* Pompton Plains, NJ: New Page Books, 2004.

Dugan, Ellen. *Garden Witch's Herbal: Green Magick, Herbalism & Spirituality.* Woodbury, MN: Llewellyn, 2009.

Dunn, Patrick. *Postmodern Magic: The Art of Magic in the Information Age.* Woodbury, MN: Llewellyn, 2005.

Ellison, Rev. Robert Lee "Skip." *Ogham: The Secret Language of the Druids.* Tucson, AZ: ADF Publishing, 2008.

Emery, Carla. *The Encyclopedia of Country Living.* Seattle, WA: Sasquatch, 2008. (*A compendium of the domestic arts of self-sufficiency.*)

Gallagher, Ann-Marie. *The Spells Bible: The Definitive Guide to Charms and Enchantments.* New York: Sterling, 2003.

———. *The Wicca Bible: The Definitive Guide to Magic and the Craft.* New York: Sterling, 2005.

Gelb, Michael J. *How to Think Like Leonardo da Vinci.* McHenry, IL: Delta, 2004. (*A wonderful book that explains da Vinci's seven-step explanation of intentional learning, creativity, and personal growth.*)

George, Demetra, and Douglas Birch. *Astrology for Yourself: How to Understand and Interpret Your Own Birth Chart.* Berwick, ME: Ibis Press, 2006. (*An excellent introductory text for those new to astrology, but detailed enough for the experienced user as well.*)

González-Whippler, Migene. *The Complete Book of Amulets and Talismans.* St. Paul, MN: Llewellyn, 1991.

Greer, John Michael. *Pagan Prayer Beads: Magic and Meditation with Pagan Rosaries.* Newburyport, MA: Weiser, 2007.

Hall, Manly K. *The Secret Teachings of All Ages.* Blacksburg, VA: Wilder, 2009. (*A gorgeous book, filled with the arcane knowledge of the ages and illustrated with striking full-color plates.*)

Harris, Eleanor, and Philip Harris. *The Crafting & Use of Ritual Tools: Step-by-Step Instructions for Woodcrafting Religious & Magical Implements.* St. Paul, MN: Llewellyn, 2002.

Henes, Donna. *Celestially Auspicious Occasions: Seasons, Cycles, & Celebrations*. New York: Perigee, 1996.

Highfield, Roger. *The Science of Harry Potter: How Magic Really Works*. New York: Penguin, 2003.

Illes, Judika. *Element Encyclopedia of Witchcraft*. London: Thorsons, 2005. (*An encyclopedic work by Illes; this one focuses on different elements of craft, correspondences, etc.*)

———. *Encyclopedia of 5000 Spells*. New York: HarperOne, 2009. (*Another encyclopedic tome of spellcraft, components, and so forth.*)

Jordan, Michael. *Ceremonies for Life*. London: Collins and Brown, 2001.

Judith, Anodea. *Chakra Balancing*. Louisville, CO: Sounds True, 2006.

Jung, C. G. *The Red Book*. New York: Norton, 2009.

K, Amber. *Ritual Craft: Creating Rites for Transformation and Celebration*. Woodbury, MN: Llewellyn, 2006.

Leslie, Clare Walker, and Charles E. Roth. *Keeping a Nature Journal: Discover a Whole New Way of Seeing the World Around You*. North Adams, MA: Storey, 2003.

Lippincott, Kristen. *Astronomy (DK Eyewitness Books)*. New York: DK Children, 2008. (*An image-rich guide that provides a wonderful introduction to astronomy.*)

Llewellyn's Sabbats Almanac. Woodbury, MN: Llewellyn, published annually.

Maresh, Jan Saunders. *Sewing for Dummies, 3rd edition*. Hoboken, NJ: Wiley, 2010.

MacLir, Alferian Gwydion. *Wandlore: The Art of Crafting the Ultimate Magical Tool*. Woodbury, MN: Llewellyn, 2011.

Miller, Jason. *Protection & Reversal Magick: A Witch's Defense Manual*. Pompton Plains, NJ: New Page Books, 2006.

Moore, Barbara. *Tarot for Beginners: A Practical Guide to Reading the Cards*. Woodbury, MN: Llewellyn, 2010.

Mosley, Ivo, ed. *Earth Poems: Poems from Around the World to Honor the Earth*. San Francisco: HarperSanFrancisco, 1996.

Moura, Ann. *Green Witchcraft III: The Manual*. St. Paul, MN: Llewellyn, 2000.

The Old Farmer's Almanac. Dublin, NH: Old Farmer's Almanac, published annually.

Ophir, Eyal, Clifford Nass, and Anthony D. Wagner. "Cognitive Control in Media Mul-titaskers." Proceedings of the National Academy of Sciences. July 2009. http://www.scribd.com/doc/19081547/Cognitive-control-in-media-multitaskers.

Paxson, Diana L. *Taking Up the Runes: A Complete Guide to Using Runes in Spells, Rituals, Divination, and Magic.* Newburyport, MA: Weiser, 2005.

Pellant, Chris. *Rocks and Minerals (Smithsonian Handbook).* New York: DK Adult, 2002.

Pesznecker, Susan. *Crafting Magick with Pen and Ink: Learn to Write Stories, Spells, and Other Magickal Works.* Woodbury, MN: Llewellyn, 2009.

Peterson Field Guides. Boston: Houghton Mifflin Harcourt, various years. (*These pocket guides are available for every type of natural observation—birds, trees, weather, herbs, etc.—and for many specific geological areas, too.*)

Pollan, Michael. "Michael Pollan." 2011. http://michaelpollan.com/ (*Pollan is one of America's preeminent food scholars and journalists and has written several books about food and food culture. His site includes many of his essays and writings.*)

Regardie, Israel, and Pat Zalewski. *Ceremonial Magic: A Guide to the Mechanisms of Ritual.* London: Aeon, 2008.

Roberts, Elizabeth, and Elias Amidon, eds. *Life Prayers: 365 Prayers, Blessings, and Affirmations to Celebrate the Human Journey.* San Francisco: HarperSanFrancisco, 1996.

Roney-Dougal, Serena. *Where Science and Magic Meet.* Stathe, UK: Green Magick, 2010.

Scarpa, Sandra McCraw. *Magical Fabric Art: Spellwork & Wishcraft through Patchwork Quilting and Sewing.* St. Paul, MN: Llewellyn, 1998.

Serith, Ceisiwr. *A Book of Pagan Prayer.* Newburyport, MA: Weiser, 2002. (*A lovely collection of Pagan-oriented prayers and blessings for all occasions from the casual to the celebratory.*)

Simpson, John, and Edmund Weiner, eds. *Oxford English Dictionary, second edition.* Oxford: Oxford University Press, 1989.

Smedley, Wendy. *Start Scrapbooking: Your Essential Guide to Recording Memories.* Cincinnati, OH: Memory Makers Books, 2010.

Sommer, Robin Langley. *Nota Bene: A Guide to Familiar Latin Quotes and Phrases.* New York: Barnes and Noble, 1995.

Starhawk. *The Spiral Dance: A Rebirth of the Ancient Religion of the Goddess, 20th Anniversary Edition.* New York: HarperOne, 1999.

Sullivan, Tammy. *Elemental Witch: Fire, Air, Water, Earth; Discover Your Natural Affinity.* Woodbury, MN: Llewellyn, 2006.

Telesco, Patricia. *A Kitchen Witch's Cookbook.* St. Paul, MN: Llewellyn, 2002.

———. *Exploring Candle Magick.* Pompton Plains, NJ: Career Press, 2008.

Tells, Gisela. "Multitasking Splits the Brain." *Science Magazine,* 15 April 2010. <http://news.sciencemag.org/sciencenow/2010/04/multitasking-splits-the-brain.html>

Tolkien, J. R. R. *The Lord of the Rings.* London, Allen & Unwin, 1954–55.

We'Moon: Gaia Rhythms for Womyn. Estacada, OR: Mother Tongue Ink, 2011. (*Published continually since 1980, this annual combines a datebook format with art, poetry, readings, moon lore, and astrology. Although decidedly woman-centered, it is full of wonderful magick and interpersonal insights that anyone could use.*)

Zell-Ravenheart, Oberon. *Companion for the Apprentice Wizard.* Pompton Plains, NJ: New Page Books, 2004. (*A detail-packed sequel to Zell-Ravenheart's Grimoire.*)

———. *Green Egg Omelette: An Anthology of Art and Articles from the Legendary Pagan Journal.* Pompton Plains, NJ: New Page Books, 2008.

———. *Grimoire for the Apprentice Wizard.* Pompton Plains, NJ: New Page Books, 2004. (*This book, which has been described as a "Boy Scout Handbook for magick users," is rich with "how-tos" and tables of correspondences, planetary hours, rituals, spellwork, and the like.*)

Zell-Ravenheart, Oberon, and Morning Glory Zell-Ravenheart. *Creating Circles and Ceremonies: Rituals for All Seasons and Reasons.* Pompton Plains, NJ: New Page Books, 2006.

Index

To Write to the Author

If you wish to contact the author or would like more information about this book, please write to the author in care of Llewellyn Worldwide Ltd. and we will forward your request. Both the author and publisher appreciate hearing from you and learning of your enjoyment of this book and how it has helped you. Llewellyn Worldwide Ltd. cannot guarantee that every letter written to the author can be answered, but all will be forwarded. Please write to:

Susan Pesznecker
℅ Llewellyn Worldwide
2143 Wooddale Drive
Woodbury, MN 55125-2989

Please enclose a self-addressed stamped envelope for reply,
or $1.00 to cover costs. If outside the USA, enclose
an international postal reply coupon.

Many of Llewellyn's authors have websites with additional information and resources. For more information, please visit our website at http://www.llewellyn.com.

Crafting Magick with Pen and Ink
Learn to Write Stories, Spells and Other Magickal Works

SUSAN PESZNECKER • FOREWORD BY RICHARD WEBSTER

Would you like to craft your own Book of Shadows? Create a ritual or spell for a special occasion? And ultimately infuse your writing with added beauty, style, and power? Just dip your quill into the deep wells of magick and creativity—and let the sparks of inspiration fly!

Empower your pen as you respond to the writing prompts and explore the techniques in this down-to-earth guide to magickal writing. Learn to write from the ground up with step-by-step instructions that take you through each stage of the creative process: brainstorming topics, freewriting, choosing a composition form, writing a rough draft, and revising your work to a refined polish. Sprinkled throughout are enjoyable exercises, helpful tips and terms, and inspiring writing samples to help you hone your craft. Whatever your medium—poetry, stories, spells, chants, prayers, blessings, or rituals—this book synthesizes the exciting realms of magick and writing to make your words truly come alive.

978-0-7387-1145-4, 264 pp., 6 x 9 $16.95

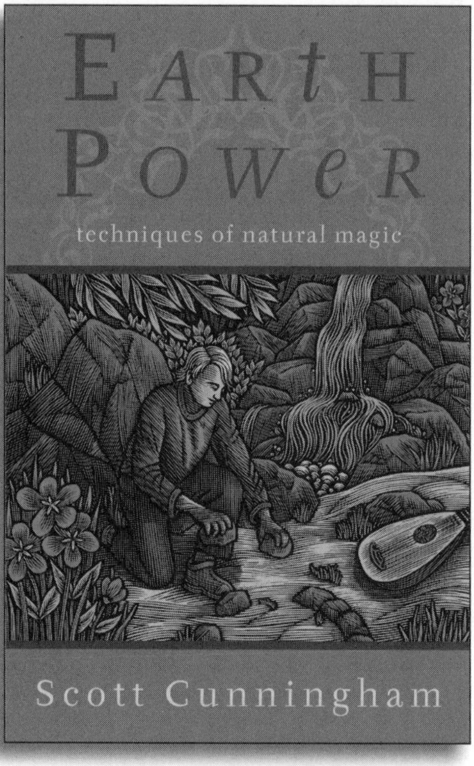
Earth Power
techniques of natural magic
Scott Cunningham

Earth Power
Techniques of Natural Magic
SCOTT CUNNINGHAM

When you draw a heart in the sand, call on the four winds for assistance, or ask the rain to wash away a bad habit, you are practicing earth magic. By working in harmony with nature, we can transform ourselves, our lives, and our world. This tried-and-true guide offers more than one hundred spells, rites, and simple rituals you can perform using the powerful energy of the earth.

978-0-87542-121-6, 192 pp., 5³⁄₁₆ x 8   **$11.95**

~ ELLEN DUGAN ~

Garden Witch's
HERBAL

Green magick,
herbalism & spirituality

FROM THE AUTHOR OF
GARDEN WITCHERY

Garden Witch's Herbal

Green Magick, Herbalism & Spirituality

ELLEN DUGAN

Enrich your Craft—and your spirit—by working with the awesome energies of nature. In this follow-up to *Garden Witchery*, Ellen Dugan takes us further down the path of green magick, revealing the secret splendors of the plant kingdom.

From common herbs and flowers to enchanted shrubs and trees, Dugan digs up the magickal dirt on a wide variety of plant life. Encouraging Witches to think outside the window box, she shares ideas for incorporating your garden's bounty into spellwork, Sabbat celebrations, and more. Tips for container gardening ensure that city Witches can get in on the green action, too.

This stimulating guide to green Witchery—featuring botanical illustrations of nearly fifty fascinating specimens—will inspire you to personalize your Craft and fortify your connection to the earth.

978-0-7387-1429-5, 336 pp., 7½ x 7½ $19.95

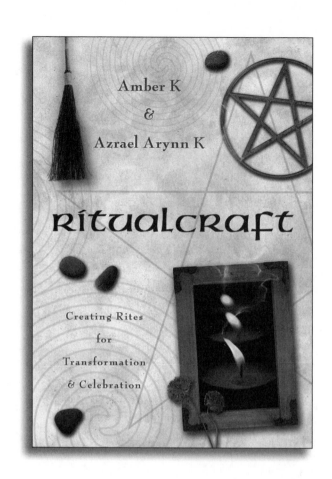

RitualCraft

Creating Rites for Transformation and Celebration

AMBER K & AZRAEL ARYNN K

From Sabbat events to magick ceremonies to handfastings, ritual is at the heart of Pagan worship and celebration. Whether you're planning a simple coven initiation or an elaborate outdoor event for hundreds, *RitualCraft* can help you create and conduct meaningful rituals.

Far from a recipe book of rote readings, this modern text explores rituals from many cultures and offers a step-by-step Neopagan framework for creating your own. The authors share their own ritual experiences—the best and the worst—illustrating the elements that contribute to successful ritual. *RitualCraft* covers all kinds of occasions: celebrations for families, a few people, or large groups; rites of passage; Esbats and Sabbats; and personal transformation. Costumes, ethics, music, physical environment, ritual tools, safety, speech, and timing are all discussed in this all-inclusive guidebook to ritual.

978-1-56718-009-1, 624 pp., 7 x 10 $29.95

To order, call 1-877-NEW-WRLD
Prices subject to change without notice
Order at Llewellyn.com 24 hours a day, 7 days a week!